Movements of Thought

Movements of Thought

Ludwig Wittgenstein's Diary, 1930–1932 and 1936–1937

Translated by Alfred Nordmann

Edited by James C. Klagge
and Alfred Nordmann

Introduction by Ray Monk

ROWMAN & LITTLEFIELD
Lanham • Boulder • New York • London

The normalized German text of the diary and the correspondence was originally edited by Ilse Somavilla.

Published by Rowman & Littlefield
An imprint of The Rowman & Littlefield Publishing Group, Inc.
4501 Forbes Boulevard, Suite 200, Lanham, Maryland 20706
www.rowman.com

86-90 Paul Street, London EC2A 4NE

British Library Cataloguing in Publication Information Available

Library of Congress Cataloging-in-Publication Data

Names: Wittgenstein, Ludwig, 1889–1951, author. | Klagge, James Carl, 1954– editor. | Nordmann, Alfred, 1956– editor translator.
Title: Movements of thought : Ludwig Wittgenstein's diary, 1930–1932 and 1936–1937 / translated by Alfred Nordmann ; edited by James C. Klagge, and Alfred Nordmann ; introduction by Ray Monk.
Other titles: Denkbewegungen. English
Description: Lanham : Rowman & Littlefield Publishers, [2023] | Translation of: Denkbewegungen: Tagebücher, 1930–1932/1936–1937, Innsbruck : Haymon, c1997. | Includes bibliographical references and index.
Identifiers: LCCN 2022034575 (print) | LCCN 2022034576 (ebook) | ISBN 9781538163665 (cloth) | ISBN 9781538163672 (paperback) | ISBN 9781538163689 (ebook)
Subjects: LCSH: Wittgenstein, Ludwig, 1889–1951—Diaries. | Philosophers—Germany—Diaries.
Classification: LCC B3376.W564 A3 2023 (print) | LCC B3376.W564 (ebook) | DDC 192—dc23/eng/20221003
LC record available at https://lccn.loc.gov/2022034575
LC ebook record available at https://lccn.loc.gov/2022034576

Contents

Editors' Preface

Wittgenstein's writing can be divided into three categories—a very few publications, a great many handwritten manuscripts, and various typescripts generated from the manuscripts. The manuscript that is translated here was handwritten over a period of seven years in a single hardbound notebook. It is unusual among Wittgenstein's manuscripts in that it contains both personal and philosophical remarks and because he did not fill it up with remarks continuously but instead he returned to it over and over on a number of different occasions. It functioned for him rather as a diary. After Wittgenstein's death in 1951, his sister, Margarete Stonborough, gave it as a personal memento to Wittgenstein's old friend Rudolf Koder (1902–1977). It remained unknown to Wittgenstein scholars until after Koder's death, and it was eventually published in German in 1997.[1]

The first portion of the diary consists of sometimes intensely personal observations from the years 1930–1932. These come from the

---

1. *Denkbewegungen: Tagebücher, 1930–1932/1936–1937*, edited by Ilse Somavilla. Koder was a schoolteacher who became friends with Wittgenstein during the time they taught elementary school in rural Austria in the 1920s. They bonded over their love of music, and their correspondence was published in *Wittgenstein und die Musik*. More details about the diary and its history can be found in the "Editorial Note," in *Wittgenstein's* Denkbewegungen *(Diaries 1930–1932/1936–1937): Interdisciplinary Perspectives*, p. 255.

time when Wittgenstein had returned to Cambridge to work again on philosophy, and they contain no coded remarks at all. The second part, observations from 1936–1937, was written in Norway, or on the way to Norway. Here we see him switching between coded and uncoded remarks in the middle of philosophical reflections, as well as personal observations. In fact, Wittgenstein subjects apparently personal concerns to the same scrutiny, the same movements of thought, the same standards of written expression as he does more overtly philosophical matters.

This translation, by Alfred Nordmann, is an attempt to render Wittgenstein's remarks as literally as possible. Much has been made of the literary value of Wittgenstein's writing. In this translation, it becomes manifest as an ongoing, not always successful, search for precision. Even at its very best, Wittgenstein's prose is never smooth or elegant. Noting that he is "in love with my sort of movement of thought in philosophy," he is quick to add: "This does not mean, by the way, that I am in love with my style."[2] He favors noun constructions, uses few adjectives, and chooses simple predicative verbs; instead of trying to express what he feels, he offers descriptions of his feelings. These descriptions are pointed and acute when they issue from exacting observation. Occasionally, however, they fail to attain clarity, perhaps because Wittgenstein has not yet attained a sufficiently clear view of a matter. And Wittgenstein sometimes settles for an awkward formulation of a thought presumably because it is the honest formulation, even when a less awkward formulation would have been available in German.

Underlined words and phrases (single or double) were underlined by Wittgenstein for emphasis. Text written in the diary using a reverse alphabet code appears here decoded and printed in italics. Often, Wittgenstein considered alternate wording or indicated uncertainty about word choices. In the interest of readability, these hesitations have not been preserved in this edition.[3]

---

2. Diary entry on October 13, 1931; p. 54, *infra*.

3. Readers interested in issues of translation or hesitations or alternate wording should consult the German and English publication of the diary in *Public and Private Occasions*, where all of these details are laid out. Readers interested in further reflections on the contents of the diary may consult Nordmann's "The Sleepy Philosopher: How to Read Wittgenstein's Diaries," and essays in *Wittgenstein's* Denkbewegungen *(Diaries 1930–1932/1936–1937): Interdisciplinary Perspectives*. We also look forward to a forthcoming book by Gabriel Citron, *The Redemption of Fragility: Wittgenstein's Struggles and Ours*, which draws heavily on this diary.

The editorial notes to the diary have been expanded and updated for this new edition. Notes deriving from Ilse Somavilla are marked with [I.S.]. The editors wish to thank Ilse Somavilla, the original editor of these texts, who produced in exemplary fashion a meticulous transcription as well as an elegantly prepared "normalized" readable German text. It is on the basis of her work that we could bring in further considerations and amendments—many arising in the process of translation, others through situating the text within more recent Wittgenstein scholarship. We also wish to thank the Department of Philosophy and the College of Liberal Arts and Human Sciences at Virginia Tech for financial support that made this new edition possible.

James C. Klagge, Virginia Tech
Alfred Nordmann, Technische Universität Darmstadt
May 2022

Introduction

Philosophy as Work on Oneself

Ray Monk

"Work on philosophy," Wittgenstein once wrote, "is really more work on oneself."[1] It was a view he held throughout his life. The work presented here shows how seriously he took this view and how integral it was to his conception both of philosophy and of himself. The diary is known to Wittgenstein scholars as the "Koder diaries," but is here published under the title *Movements of Thought: Ludwig Wittgenstein's Diary, 1930–1932 and 1936–1937*. Central to the diary is the theme of vanity and how this, if unchecked, will lead to a kind of dishonesty that is corrosive both of clear thinking and moral decency. Purging or, as Wittgenstein liked sometimes to put it, "dismantling" this vanity was the goal of the work on himself in which he was engaged during this period, and the way in which he chose to pursue that purgatory task was through *confession*. To understand the "movements of thought" that led him along this path, it helps, I think, to see them in the context of Wittgenstein's life as a whole, thereby to appreciate the extent to which thinking clearly and striving for moral decency were, for him, *always* inextricably linked, two sides of a single task.

The subtitle of my biography of him, "The Duty of Genius," alludes to this view and to the way it is formulated in a book that

---

1. *Culture and Value*, p. 16 (1980 edition)/p. 24 (1998 revised edition); October 14, 1931.

Wittgenstein read as a young man and acknowledged, throughout his life, as a formative influence: *Sex and Character* by Otto Weininger. *Sex and Character* is, in many ways, a strange book. Much of what it says about women, Jews, and homosexuals is deeply offensive and, as Wittgenstein was to acknowledge, plainly wrong.[2] What was to have a profound influence on Wittgenstein, however, were not those disturbingly misguided views but rather Weininger's conception of the duties that men have by virtue of being moral beings. All men, Weininger believed, have an obligation to strive to become the very highest type of man: the genius. Genius, Weininger writes, "is the highest morality, and, therefore, it is everyone's duty."[3] This duty has two aspects: thinking clearly and behaving decently. Thus, according to Weininger, logic and ethics are fundamentally the same: "They are no more than duty to oneself."[4] They are, so to speak, two sides of the single duty of genius.

Versions of this thought occur repeatedly throughout Wittgenstein's life and work. To give a notable example, we can see it exerting a powerful influence on him when he first decided to devote himself to philosophy. Such a decision could be justified, he believed, only if he had the potential to make an absolutely first-rate contribution to the subject, if, that is, philosophy was something for which he had not only talent but also genius. His passionate, all-consuming interest in philosophy began while he was studying aeronautical engineering at the University of Manchester. After reading Bertrand Russell's book *The Principles of Mathematics*, he became preoccupied with the questions left unresolved by Russell's work, questions to do with the nature of logic. He thought the resolution of these problems might just provide him with a chance to develop his own genius. Whether this was true or not was a question that burned to the very depths of his soul, and he found himself incapable of thinking about anything else. As his sister Hermine describes it, "philosophy, or rather reflection on philosophical problems, suddenly became such an obsession with him, and took hold of him so completely against his will, that he suffered terribly, feeling torn between conflicting vocations." "During this time," she

---

2. See letter to G. E. Moore, August 23, 1931, *Wittgenstein in Cambridge*, p. 193.
3. *Sex and Character*, p. 159.
4. Ibid., p. 139.

adds, "Ludwig was in a constant, indescribable, almost pathological state of agitation."[5]

Eventually, as if he can stand it no longer, in October 1911, Wittgenstein traveled to Cambridge to attend Russell's lectures and to discuss philosophy with him. At the end of that term, he asked Russell whether he should continue with philosophy or return to aeronautics. Russell asked him to write something over the vacation so that he could form a judgment. When he read what Wittgenstein had written, Russell was extremely impressed and advised him to abandon his aeronautical studies in favor of philosophy. "Perhaps," he wrote to his lover, Ottoline Morrell, "he will do great things."[6] The following summer, Russell told Wittgenstein's sister Hermine, "We expect the next big step in philosophy to be taken by your brother." He later described Wittgenstein as "perhaps the most perfect example I have ever known of genius as traditionally conceived."[7] For his part, Wittgenstein told his friend David Pinsent that Russell's recognition of his genius had, quite literally, saved his life, ending nine years of loneliness and suffering, during which he had repeatedly thought of suicide. It enabled him finally to give up engineering and to brush aside "a hint that he was *de trop* in this world,"[8] a hint that had made him feel ashamed that he had *not* killed himself. At last, he was able to feel that he had a task worth pursuing, one that would potentially enable him to realize the genius within him, thereby giving meaning and purpose to his life.

In the following years, Russell continued to be impressed by Wittgenstein and came to regard him as his natural heir in philosophy. However, like most subsequent philosophers who came to name Wittgenstein as an influence, he failed to realize, or at least to take fully seriously, the fact that, for Wittgenstein, thinking clearly was only one part of his philosophical task, the other being the overcoming of moral defects. Russell liked to tell the story of how, when Wittgenstein came to his rooms in Trinity College to discuss philosophy, he would pace up and down in silence. Once, Russell asked: "Are you thinking about logic or your sins?" "Both," replied Wittgenstein and continued his pacing.[9]

5. *Recollections of Wittgenstein*, p. 2.
6. BR to OM, January 23, 1912, *Ludwig Wittgenstein: Duty of Genius*, p. 41.
7. Russell, *Autobiography*, vol. 2, p. 136.
8. *Ludwig Wittgenstein: Duty of Genius*, p. 41.
9. Russell, *Autobiography*, vol. 2, p. 137.

During this time, and, in fact, throughout the time of their friend-ship, Russell repeatedly failed to understand the nature of Witt-genstein's preoccupation with his own "sins." Thanks to his habit of writing to his lover Ottoline Morrell many times a day, several instances of this have been recorded. In one of his letters to Mor-rell, for example, he described Wittgenstein as "far more terrible with Christians than I am," citing, as an example, Wittgenstein's fierce reaction to meeting someone he refers to only as "F. the un-dergraduate monk" (from the diaries of Wittgenstein's friend David Pinsent, we learn that the "F" stands for "Farmer"). According to Russell, Wittgenstein had initially liked Farmer and was horrified to discover that he was a monk. Upon discovering this, Wittgen-stein attacked him "with absolute fury," not *arguing* against his faith "but only preaching honesty. He abominates ethics and morals generally."[10]

Two misunderstandings strike one about Russell's account. The first is his assumption that what Wittgenstein was objecting to was Christianity itself when it is clear that his horror was more focused on his conviction that this student could not *in all honesty* become a monk. It was Farmer's spiritual well-being that Wittgenstein was concerned with, not the truth or otherwise of his beliefs (hence his lack of argumentation). Secondly, that concern with honesty surely suggests that, far from *abominating* morality, Wittgenstein was expressing a moral point of view, one based on the fundamental importance of avoiding insincerity and dishonesty.

That Wittgenstein had more sympathy for Christianity and for religion in general than Russell had supposed became clear (or, any-way, should have become clear) when, one day in the early summer of 1912, he surprised Russell by saying how much he admired the text (taken from St. Mark's Gospel 8:36), "What shall it profit a man if he gain the whole world and lose his own soul." He went on to say how few there are who do *not* lose their souls.[11] A few months later, he wrote to Russell that he had been reading *Varieties of Religious Experience* by William James. "This book," he told Russell, "does me a *lot* of good."[12]

If maintaining ruthlessly strict standards of honesty and integrity was one thing required to avoid losing one's soul, the other was

10. BR to OM, March 7, 1912, *Ludwig Wittgenstein: Duty of Genius*, p. 44.
11. BR to OM, May 30, 1912, *Ludwig Wittgenstein: Duty of Genius*, p. 51.
12. *Wittgenstein in Cambridge*, p. 30; June 22, 1912.

doing everything one could to produce a work of genius, putting *everything* else to one side. Wittgenstein's exemplar in this respect was Beethoven. One day, he told Russell how a friend of Beethoven's once described going to Beethoven's home and hearing him "cursing, howling and singing" over his new fugue. After an hour, Beethoven came to the door looking as if he had been fighting the devil and having eaten nothing for 36 hours because his cook and parlor-maid had been frightened away by his rage. "That's the sort of man to be," Wittgenstein insisted.[13]

How seriously Wittgenstein took this was illustrated by an occasion that took place in November 1912, near the start of Wittgenstein's second year at Cambridge, when Russell took him to watch a rowing race on the river in which North Whitehead, the son of Russell's friend and colleague, Alfred Whitehead, was competing. Wittgenstein, Russell reported to his lover Ottoline Morrell, found the whole thing *disgusting*. After a brief, heated exchange on the subject, Wittgenstein "suddenly stood still and explained that the way we had spent the afternoon was so vile that we ought not to live, or at least he ought not, that nothing is tolerable except producing great works or enjoying those of others, that he has accomplished nothing and never will, etc."[14]

In the summer of 1913, after a brief holiday in Norway with David Pinsent, Wittgenstein announced to both Pinsent and Russell that he wished to return there by himself to devote himself to his work on logic. In his diary, Pinsent records Wittgenstein as giving as a reason for this that he had no right to live in an antipathetic world surrounded by people for whom he felt contempt "without some justification for that contempt etc., such as being a really great man and having done really great work."[15]

The letters he sent to Russell from Norway combine updates on his progress in thinking about logic with reflections on himself. "Deep inside me," he wrote, "there's a perpetual seething, like the bottom of a geyser, and I keep hoping that things will come to an eruption once and for all, so that I can turn into a different person." Anticipating that Russell would not readily understand this desire for self-transformation or the importance it had for him, Wittgenstein added: "Perhaps you regard this thinking about myself as a

---

13. BR to OM, April 23, 1912, *Ludwig Wittgenstein: Duty of Genius*, p. 45.
14. BR to OM, November 9, 1912, *Ludwig Wittgenstein: Duty of Genius*, p. 65.
15. *Ludwig Wittgenstein: Duty of Genius*, p. 89.

waste of time—but how can I be a logician before I'm a human be-ing! *Far* the most important thing is to settle accounts with myself!"[16]

In the New Year of 1914, Russell discovered that one of the things Wittgenstein wanted to do to settle accounts with himself and turn into a different person was to sever relations with him. In what was clearly intended to be his last letter to Russell, Wittgenstein told him: "We've often had uncomfortable conversations with one another when certain subjects came up. And the uncomfortableness was not a consequence of ill humour on one side or the other but of enormous differences in our natures." "*I shall not write to you again,*" he added, "*and you will not see me again either.*"[17] Russell replied to this with such tact and kindness that Wittgenstein did, after all, write again, explaining that he thought his and Russell's ideals were so different that "we shan't *ever* be able to talk about anything in-volving our value-judgements without either becoming hypocritical or falling out."[18] The unspoken but doubtless implicit line of reason-ing was surely this: Wittgenstein had come to Norway to produce a work of philosophy of the very first rank. As this required not only clarity of thought but also utter honesty, it was incompatible with the kind of hypocrisy that would be required if he and Russell were to remain friends. He suggested a compromise: "Let's write to each other about our work, our health, and the like, but let's avoid in our communications any kind of value-judgement,"[19] a plan to which he adhered for the remainder of his correspondence with Russell.

Wittgenstein intended to remain in Norway, untainted by friend-ships that required compromising his fundamental values, until he had finished the work on philosophy that, he hoped, would provide a definitive answer to the question: "What is logic?" However, when he returned to Vienna in July 1914, he found that his plan to return to Norway after a brief holiday with David Pinsent was thwarted by the outbreak of the First World War. Wittgenstein's reaction was to enlist in the Austrian army, not, like his brothers Paul and Kurt, as an officer but instead as an ordinary private in an artillery regiment. Reading his diaries of the time, it is difficult to resist the conclusion that he did so as a consequence of his desire to "turn into a different person." In *Varieties of Religious Experience*, the book that Wittgen-

---

16. *Wittgenstein in Cambridge*, p. 63.
17. Ibid., p. 68.
18. Ibid., p. 71; March 3, 1914.
19. Idem.

stein had told Russell "does me a *lot* of good," William James writes: "No matter what a man's frailties otherwise may be, if he be willing to risk death, and still more if he suffer it heroically, in the service he has chosen, this fact consecrates him forever."[20] Echoing this, on the first day that Wittgenstein caught his first glance of the enemy, the Russian army, he wrote: "Now I have the chance to be a decent human being for I'm standing eye to eye with death."[21]

A month into the war, Wittgenstein bought from a bookshop in Galicia, where he was stationed, *The Gospel in Brief* by Leo Tolstoy. This was to have an utterly transformative effect. He read it so often that he knew whole passages of it by heart and became known to his comrades as "the man with the gospels." "If you are not acquainted with it," he wrote to the publisher Ludwig von Ficker, whom he had gotten to know in Vienna, "then you cannot imagine what an effect it can have upon a person."[22] From it, he acquired the view that "Christianity is indeed the only *sure* way to happiness,"[23] not because its tenets were *true* but rather because the figure of Jesus Christ, as described in the gospels, offered an example, a model, of how to be a "decent human being."

Wittgenstein had taken with him to the Russian Front his philosophical notebooks and, when he could, he continued to write about logic and language. He also wrote personal remarks, some of them spiritual exhortations and religious reflections, some more in the nature of a diary of day-to-day events. These personal remarks were written in a code that he had learned as a child (the same one used in the Koder diary). However, in June 1916, in the thick of the Brusilov offensive on the Russian Front, Wittgenstein wrote: "What do I know about God and the purpose of life?" and answered with a list of propositions that show clearly the influence of Tolstoy (e.g., "The meaning of life, i.e. the meaning of the world, we can call God," "To pray is to think about the meaning of life").[24] These remarks were *not* written in code but rather presented as if they belonged to the writings on logic and language that precede them. It is as if thinking about philosophy and religion, logic and his sins, had finally come together to form a single "movement of thought."

---

20. *Varieties of Religious Experience*, p. 364; Lectures XIV and XV.
21. *Ludwig Wittgenstein: Duty of Genius*, p. 112.
22. Ibid., p. 116.
23. Ibid., p. 123.
24. Ibid., pp. 140–41.

Before the war, while still in Norway, Wittgenstein had drawn a distinction between what can be *said* in language and what is unsayable but nevertheless can be *shown*. The cause of many confusions about logic, he believed, was a failure to recognize the limits of language, a failure, in particular, to realize that logic is "ineffable." It is impossible to say anything about logical form, but it *can* be shown. Now, he applied that distinction to religion and the meaning of life:

> The solution to the problem of life is to be seen in the disappearance of the problem.
>
> Isn't this the reason why men to whom the meaning of life had become clear after long doubting could not say what this meaning consisted in?[25]

Late in 1916, while in Olmütz, Moravia, to be trained as an officer, Wittgenstein became friends with a young architect named Paul Engelmann, who sympathized with, and indeed shared, Wittgenstein's thoughts on the ineffability of ethical and religious truths. Discussions with Engelmann helped Wittgenstein to finish his book on philosophy, which, by the summer of 1918, was complete. Published four years later as *Tractatus Logico-Philosophicus*, it is a curiously hybrid work. The greater part of it is taken up with articulating a theory of logic and language that attempts to present a definitive solution to the problems that had troubled Russell, but, towards the end, it includes a few remarks about "the mystical," the things that cannot be put into words. These include the truths of ethics, religion, logic, and philosophy, in all of which the solution "is to be seen in the disappearance of the problem."

Like many Austrian soldiers, Wittgenstein was held in an Italian prisoner-of-war camp for nearly a year after the war. There, he met Ludwig Hänsel, the recipient of the confessional letters included in the Appendix. Like Engelmann, Hänsel was someone with whom Wittgenstein could discuss not only philosophy in its narrow sense but also personal matters of faith and morality.

When Wittgenstein finally returned to Vienna, one of the first things he did was to divest himself of the enormous fortune he had inherited from his father, who had invested wisely, thereby protecting much of his vast fortune from the ravages of war. "Give away all

---

25. *Tractatus Logico-Philosophicus*, 6.521

that you have,"[26] advises Leo Tolstoy in *The Gospel in Brief*, for "there is no way to be rich and to fulfil your father's will."[27] It was advice Wittgenstein took to heart. "A hundred times," his sister Hermine remembers, "he wanted to assure himself that there was no possibility of any money still belonging to him in any shape or form. To the despair of the notary carrying out the transfer, he returned to this point again and again."[28] The family and the notary wanted to put aside some of the money so that Wittgenstein could have access to it if he should ever change his mind, but eventually, Wittgenstein was granted his wish to be rid of all his inheritance once and for all. "So," sighed the notary, "you want to commit financial suicide."[29]

That year Wittgenstein thought of committing actual suicide many times. He was deeply grief stricken by the news that his friend David Pinsent had been killed toward the end of the war, he felt acutely the decline of Austria after the war from a leading part of one of the great empires and cultural centers of Europe to a small, insignificant country, and, having decided to become a teacher, he found himself—a thirty-year-old war veteran—attending lectures at the teacher training college in a class of teenagers. "The humiliation is *so* great for me that often I think I can hardly bear it,"[30] he told Engelmann. He was also depressed to discover that, having finished a book he considered to have provided definitive solutions to the problems of philosophy, he could not find a publisher for it. No less than five publishers turned him down before Russell managed to find both a German and an English publisher ready to take it on but only after Russell himself had agreed to write an introduction to it explaining its importance. In May 1920, he wrote to Engelmann, "I have sunk to my lowest point."[31]

Though there were several external reasons for Wittgenstein's unhappiness during this time, he was nevertheless inclined to think that the mere fact that he was unhappy was a sign that there was something wrong with *him*. As he put it to Engelmann: "If I am unhappy and know that my unhappiness reflects a gross discrepancy between myself and life as it is, I solved nothing . . . I shall never

---

26. *The Gospel in Brief*, p. 111.
27. Ibid., p. 74.
28. *Recollections*, p. 4.
29. Ibid., p. 215.
30. *Ludwig Wittgenstein: Duty of Genius*, p. 172.
31. Ibid., p. 184.

find a way out of the chaos of my emotions and thoughts so long as I have not achieved the supreme and crucial insight that that discrepancy is not the fault of life as it is, but of myself as I am."[32] Like much else that Wittgenstein said and wrote at this time, it echoes thoughts expressed by *The Gospel in Brief*. "Nothing can defile a person from the outside," Tolstoy writes there, "only what he thinks can defile a person."[33]

In response to Wittgenstein's despair about himself, Engelmann made an intriguing suggestion, one based on his own experience and one that Wittgenstein was to act on many years later and to discuss in the documents collected in this volume. Engelmann told Wittgenstein he had been worried recently about his motives for his own work, whether they were decent and honest. To deal with this, he wrote, "I took down a kind of 'confession' in which I tried to recall the series of events in my life, in as much detail as possible in the space of an hour. With each event I tried to make clear to myself how I should have behaved. By means of such a general over-view the confused picture was much simplified."[34]

The seed sown by this idea would take about ten years to germinate, most of which Wittgenstein spent as a schoolteacher in the countryside of lower Austria. During his time as a teacher, *Tractatus Logico-Philosophicus* was published, and within a short time, it came to be greatly admired by some of the leading philosophers of the day, particularly those based in Cambridge and Vienna. Wittgenstein, meanwhile, was struggling as a teacher. His exacting standards proved too much for most of his pupils and, with a few notable exceptions, his intense manner and dominating personality alienated the villagers and his fellow teachers. Chief among those exceptions was Rudolf Koder, a music teacher who remained Wittgenstein's friend for the rest of his life. When Wittgenstein died, the diary published in the first part of this collection was given to Koder, which is why it has become known as the "Koder diary."

One of the young philosophers at Cambridge who took a special interest in the *Tractatus* was Frank Ramsey, who did most of the work in translating it into English. So taken was he with the book that Ramsey arranged to visit Wittgenstein in Puchberg, the small Austrian village in which he was then teaching, in order to discuss

---

32. Ibid., p. 185.
33. *The Gospel in Brief*, p. 14.
34. *Ludwig Wittgenstein: Duty of Genius*, p. 186.

it sentence by sentence. Ramsey's visit was fortuitous in many ways, not least of which was that it opened the door to Wittgenstein returning to philosophy and to Cambridge, which he did in the New Year of 1929.

Though there was much in the *Tractatus* that Wittgenstein was to abandon in his later philosophy, his insistence that clear thinking had to go hand-in-hand with "work on oneself" remained constant. Because, however, there is so little mention of this latter in his philosophical writings, the importance it had for him has been little understood. Various attempts have been made to correct this, including the publication by his friends of memoirs and notes of conversations that abound with moral and religious reflections. Maurice Drury, who became a close friend and confidant of Wittgenstein's soon after his arrival back in Cambridge in 1929, explained his decision to publish his own notes of conversations with Wittgenstein by saying that it was to counteract the effect of "well-meaning commentators" who "make it appear that his writings were easily assimilable into the very intellectual milieu they were largely a warning against."[35]

Soon after his return to Cambridge, Wittgenstein gave a paper to the Heretics club that came to be called the "Lecture on Ethics," which might be regarded as an explanation for why he said so little about the subject in his philosophical work, even though he regarded it as the most important aspect of that work. To attempt to say anything about ethics, he told his audience, is to "run against the boundaries of language."[36] Try as we might, we cannot cross those boundaries. "Ethics so far as it springs from the desire to say something about the meaning of life, the absolute good, the absolute valuable, can be no science. What it says does not add to our knowledge in any sense."[37] When it comes to being a decent person, what counts is not what one *says* but what one *does*. "*Im Anfang war die Tat,*" in the beginning was the deed, as Goethe put it, subverting the first line of St. John's Gospel. It was a remark that Wittgenstein considered using as a motto for his later work.

In the autumn of 1930, Wittgenstein was already thinking of producing a book outlining his later philosophy, and he wrote a series of drafts of a foreword in which he tried to make clear the *spirit* in which he wrote and how that differed from the spirit of our times,

---

35. *Recollections*, p. xi.
36. *Ludwig Wittgenstein: Duty of Genius*, p. 277.
37. Idem.

the "intellectual milieu" to which Drury refers in the remark quoted earlier. In one such draft he wrote, "It is all one to me whether or not the typical western scientist understands or appreciates my work, since he will not in any case understand the spirit in which I write."[38] In another, the final version, he struck a more explicitly religious note:

> I would like to say "This book is written to the glory of God," but, nowadays that would be chicanery, that is, it would not be rightly understood. It means the book is written in good will, and in so far as it is not so written, but out of vanity, etc., the author would wish to see it condemned. He cannot free it of these impurities further than he himself is free of them.[39]

The last sentence gets to the heart of the matter, as far as Wittgenstein was concerned: Unless he could free himself from vanity, his work would always be marred by it.

Around this time, Wittgenstein conceived the idea of writing an autobiography as one way of identifying the "impurities" of which he speaks in the preface quoted above. It is an idea possibly inspired by Weininger, who writes in *Sex and Character*: "Putting together a complete autobiography, when the need to do this originates in the man himself, is always the sign of a superior human being. For in the really faithful memory the root of piety lies."[40]

"The spirit in which one can write the truth about oneself," Wittgenstein wrote towards the end of 1929, "can take the most varied forms; from the most decent to the most indecent. And accordingly it is very desirable or very wrong for it to be written." There was something inside him, he went on, that spoke in favor of writing an autobiography that would lay out his life clearly: "Not so much to put it on trial as to produce, in any case, clarity and truth."[41]

The Koder diary contains many interesting remarks about how Wittgenstein thought about this way of attaining clarity and truth. "One could say of an autobiography," he writes in 1931, "one of the damned is writing this from hell."[42] He evidently, however, did not find it easy. Repeatedly we find in these diaries reflections such

---

38. *Culture and Value*, p. 7/p. 9.
39. *Philosophical Remarks*, preface.
40. *Sex and Character*, p. 110; *Recollections*, p. 182.
41. *Ludwig Wittgenstein: Duty of Genius*, pp. 281–82.
42. See the diary entry for October 12, 1931; p. 53, *infra*.

as: "How difficult it is to know oneself, to honestly admit what one is!"[43]

This last remark was written in Norway. In 1936, just as he had in 1913, Wittgenstein decided to live alone by the Sognefjord in order to bring his philosophical work to completion. And, again, just as during the previous occasion, this involved much self-examination and reflection, a fascinating record of which dominates the 1936–1937 section of the Koder diary. During that year, perhaps remembering what Engelmann had told him many years previously, he decided that what was necessary to "honestly admit what one is" was not (or, at least, not only) an autobiography but nothing less than a *confession*. It is easy, of course, to see how one can evolve into another. Indeed, especially on Wittgenstein's understanding of the matter, an autobiography is itself a kind of confession. In 1931, while he was still thinking of writing an autobiography, he wrote: "The conscience burdened by guilt could easily confess: but the vain person cannot confess."[44]

An autobiography addresses an audience that can remain anonymous, but a confession is made *to* someone. The first person Wittgenstein chose to receive his confession was Ludwig Hänsel, in the letter that is reproduced and translated here in the Appendix. The particular sin to which Wittgenstein confesses there is that of lying about the extent of his Jewish ancestry. While they were prisoners together, Wittgenstein wrote to Hänsel, "I said that I was descended one quarter from Jews and three quarters from Aryans, even though it is just the other way round."[45] Though this untruth had been playing on Wittgenstein's mind since his imprisonment in 1919, one can imagine it acquired a new importance in September 1935 with the passing of the Nuremberg Laws, which defined a Jew precisely as someone who had at least three Jewish grandparents.

It was not, however, the only sin to which he confessed that winter. In the Christmas period of 1936, Wittgenstein visited Cambridge and made his confession in person to, among others, Maurice Drury, G. E. Moore, Fania Pascal, his lover Francis Skinner, and his friend and ex-student Rowland Hutt. Hutt has remembered that one of the sins was relatively trifling. On being told of the death of an American acquaintance, Wittgenstein had reacted as if it had been

---

43. See the diary entry for March 12, 1937; p, 96, *infra*.
44. See the diary entry for November 2, 1931; p. 59, *infra*.
45. See Wittgenstein's letter to Hänsel dated November 7, 1936; p. 115, *infra*.

news, whereas, in fact, he had already heard of the death. Another concerned a time in the war when Wittgenstein was commanded to carry some bombs across an unsteady plank over a stream. Initially, he had been too afraid to do it. He overcame his fear, but his cowardice had haunted him ever since. Yet another is remembered in Hutt's words as: "Most people would think that I have had no relationship with women, but I have."[46]

Fania Pascal remembers the confession about the extent of his Jewishness and also another one about the time that Wittgenstein was a schoolteacher and lied about having hit one of his pupils. In fact, Wittgenstein hit several of his pupils, and there is some evidence that this was the sin of which he was most ashamed. He went to the length of returning to the village in which he had taught to apologize in person to the children he had struck.

What is common to all the misdeeds to which he confessed is dishonesty and cowardice. He evidently thought that if he could bring himself to acknowledge and confess these things, he could overcome the personal defects that, left unchecked, would disfigure his philosophical writing. "What is it?" Fania Pascal remembers exclaiming during Wittgenstein's recitation of his sins, "You want to be perfect?" "*Of course* I want to be perfect,"[47] Wittgenstein replied.

In the documents published here, scrupulously edited and translated, one gains an insight into what it is like to seek perfection in both work and character in the writings of someone convinced that these were but two parts of a single task.

---

46. *Ludwig Wittgenstein: Duty of Genius*, p. 369.
47. *Recollections*, p. 37.

Movements of
Thought Diary

Ludwig Wittgenstein returned to Cambridge and academic life in January of 1929. John Maynard Keynes reported to his wife: "God has arrived. I met him on the 5.15 train."[1] In October, Wittgenstein accepted an invitation to give his first course of lectures on "Philosophy," which began on January 20, 1930. After spending most of his Easter vacation between terms in Vienna dictating a summary of his recent philosophical views, he visited Bertrand Russell for a day and a half in Cornwall to discuss this work. Wittgenstein's fellowship at Trinity College would soon expire, and Russell was tasked with assessing his progress for the renewal of the fellowship. Wittgenstein arrived back in Cambridge on April 25, with classes to begin again on April 28. On April 26, 1930, Wittgenstein turned forty-one years old.[2]

---

1. Letter of January 18, 1929, in Monk, *Ludwig Wittgenstein: The Duty of Genius*, p. 255. See also the first letter from Wittgenstein to Hänsel, reporting on his arrival in Cambridge; p. 112, *infra*.

2. The circumstances of the preceding days are described in Monk, pp. 291–94.

1930

26.4.30

Without a little courage one can't even write a sensible remark about oneself.

Sometimes I think[3]

I suffer from a sort of mental[4] constipation. Or is that my imagination, similar to when one feels one might vomit when, in fact, there is nothing left?[5]

I am very often or almost always full of anxiety.

My brain is very irritable. Received handkerchiefs for my birthday from Marguerite today.[6] They pleased me though any word would have pleased me more & a kiss yet much more.[7]

Of all the people now alive the loss of her would hit me the hardest; I don't want to say that frivolously, for I love her or hope that I love her.

---

3. Wittgenstein appears to have added this incomplete sentence later on, perhaps to preface the following remark ("Sometimes I think I suffer . . ."). However, he did not make the corresponding adjustment of beginning the next line in lowercase. Thus, it is also possible that these words begin a sentence that was neither completed nor deleted. [I.S.]

4. Notoriously, "*Geist*" can be translated either as "mind" or as "spirit." Did Georg Wilhelm Friedrich Hegel, for example, write a phenomenology of the mind or of the spirit? Except in those few instances where the English language clearly requires "spirit" or "spiritual," "*Geist*" and "*geistig*" are rendered as "mind" and "mental."

5. Cf. Boltzmann, p. 197: "The wish to produce something when nothing further can be produced I compared . . . with the nausea under migraine where one also has the urge to throw up something when nothing is left inside."

6. Marguerite Respinger was born in 1904 and died Marguerite de Chambrier in 2000. Her father was a wealthy Swiss businessman. A Cambridge acquaintance of Wittgenstein's nephew, Thomas Stonborough, she was invited by Wittgenstein's sister Margarete to stay at their homes in Vienna and Gmunden in 1926. Soon after her arrival in Vienna, Marguerite got to know Ludwig Wittgenstein. Since he had sprained his ankle and was taken care of in his sister's house, her guest room was needed for him. In Vienna, Marguerite attended a women's school for graphic design. Later, she took a six-month course of instruction at a Vienna hospital and continued at the Red Cross school in Berne. [I.S.] Compare Monk, pp. 238–40. In the mid-1920s, Wittgenstein sculpted a bust of a young girl that seems to have been modelled on Respinger. It was long in the possession of Wittgenstein's sister Margarete and was auctioned by the Palais Dorotheum in 2017 for €109,239.

7. Writing in the coded script he often used for private remarks, Wittgenstein had noted the following on the previous day in MS 108: "Arrived in Cambridge again after my Easter vacation. In Vienna much with Marguerite. Easter Sunday in Neuwaldegg with her. We kissed each other a lot for three hours and it was very nice" (*Wiener Ausgabe*, vol. 2, p. 242). [I.S.]

I am tired & lack ideas, that is of course always the case in the first few days after my arrival until I get used to the climate. But that isn't to say, of course, that I am not standing at the beginning of an empty period.

It always strikes me frightfully when I think how entirely my profession depends on a gift which might be withdrawn from me at any moment. I think of that very often, again and again, & generally how everything can be withdrawn from one & one doesn't even know what all one <u>has</u> & only just then becomes aware of the most essential when one suddenly loses it. And one doesn't notice it precisely because it is so essential, therefore so ordinary. Just as one doesn't notice one's breathing until one has bronchitis & sees that what one considered self-evident is not so self-evident at all. And there are many more kinds of mental bronchitis.

Often I feel that there is something in me like a lump which, were it to melt, would let me cry or I would then find the right words (or perhaps even a melody). But this something (is it the heart?) in my case feels like leather & cannot melt. Or is it only that I am too much a coward to let the temperature rise sufficiently?

There are people who are too weak to vomit.[8] I am one of them.

The only thing that at some point might break in me & I am sometimes afraid of that, is my intellect.

Sometimes I think that at some point my brain won't take the strain on it & will give out. And given what its strength is, it is frightfully strained—at least that's how it often seems to me.

27.[4.30]

Until about the 23rd year of my life it would have been impossible for me to sleep in a freestanding bed & even then only with my face toward the wall. I don't know when that fear left me. Was it only during the war?

A couple of days ago I dreamt the following:

I was leading a mule whose keeper I seemed to be. First on a street—I think in an oriental town; then into an office where I had to wait in a large room. In front of that was a smaller one full of people. The mule was restless & stubborn. I held it by a short rope & thought that I would like for it to run its head up against the wall—

---

8. "*Brechen*" is the German word for "to vomit." It also means "to break." Wittgenstein shifts to this second meaning of "*brechen*" in the following remark.

at which I was sitting—then it would calm down. I kept talking to it, calling it "inspector." For it seemed to me that this was the ordinary name for a mule just as one calls a horse "bay" or a cat "kitty."[9] And I thought "if I now come to have horses I will call them inspector, too" (that is, I am so used to the word inspector from dealing with mules). Only after I awoke from this did I notice that one doesn't call mules "inspector" at all.

Ramsey's mind repulsed me.[10] When I came to Cambridge 15 months ago I thought that I would not be able to have dealings with him, for I had such unpleasant memories of him from our last meeting 4 years ago with Keynes in Sussex.[11] But Keynes, whom I told this, said to me he thought that I should well be able to talk with him & not just about logic. And I found Keynes's opinion confirmed. For I could communicate quite well with R. about some things. But in the course of time it did not really go well, after all. R's incapacity for genuine enthusiasm or genuine reverence, which is the same, finally repulsed me more & more. On the other hand I had a certain awe of R. He was a very swift & deft critic when one presented him with ideas. But his criticism didn't help along but held back & sobered. That short period of time, as Schopenhauer calls it, between the two long ones when some truth appears first paradoxical & then trivial

---

9. Instead of "cat" and "kitty," the German has "*schwein* (pig)" and "*wuz*."

10. Frank Plumpton Ramsey had died about six weeks earlier on January 19, 1930; on February 22, he would have turned twenty-seven. Wittgenstein visited him at his deathbed. Ramsey was a logician and mathematician. Following Whitehead and Russell's *Principia Mathematica*, and influenced by Wittgenstein's analysis of tautologies, Ramsey attempted to provide a logical foundation for mathematics. He also considered the logic of decision and questions of national economy. In September of 1923, he visited Wittgenstein for two weeks in Puchberg, where they read and discussed the *Tractatus* daily. In October of 1923, Ramsey's review of the *Tractatus* appeared in the philosophical journal *Mind*. [I.S.] In the year that preceded his death, Ramsey "was not only Wittgenstein's most valued partner in philosophical discussion, but also his closest friend" (Monk, p. 258; also p. 498). Wittgenstein acknowledged Ramsey's "always certain and forcible" criticism in his preface to the *Philosophical Investigations*. See also Wittgenstein's comments on Ramsey from 1931, in *Culture and Value*, p. 17/24; November 1, 1931.

11. Wittgenstein had come to know John Maynard Keynes (1883–1946) in 1912 during his studies with Russell. Wittgenstein was to join them as a member of the "Apostles" but did not feel comfortable about this and wanted to submit his resignation a few days after his election. Even though there was no close friendship between Wittgenstein and Keynes, he could always count on help from the prominent economist and founder of "Keynesianism." [I.S.] As a matter of fact (see Monk, pp. 230–31), the meeting had taken place five years ago.

to people, had shrunk to a point for R.[12] And so at first one labored arduously for a long time in vain to explain something to him until he suddenly shrugged his shoulders about it & said this was self-evident, after all. But he wasn't insincere about this. He had an ugly <u>mind</u>. But not an ugly soul.[13] He truly relished music & with understanding. And one could see by looking at him what effect it had on him. Of the last movement of one of Beethoven's last quartets, a movement he loved perhaps more than anything else, he told me that it made him feel as if the heavens were open. And that meant something when he said it.[14]

Freud surely errs very frequently & as far as his character is concerned he is probably a swine or something similar, but in what he says there is a great deal.[15] And the same is true of me. There is a <u>lot</u> in what I say.[16]

I like dawdling. Perhaps less so now than in former times.

28.[4.30]

I often think that the highest I wish to achieve would be to compose a melody. Or it mystifies me that in the desire for this, none ever

---

12. Near the end of his preface to the first edition of *The World as Will and Representation*, Arthur Schopenhauer speaks of the fate that always befalls the knowledge of truth, "to which only a brief triumph is allotted between the two long periods in which it is condemned as paradoxical or disparaged as trivial." [I.S.]

13. For his part, Ramsey had the following to say about Wittgenstein in a letter in 1929: "He is . . . very nice, but rather dogmatic and inclined to repeat explanations of simple things. Because if you doubt the truth of what he says he always thinks you can't have understood. This makes him rather tiring to talk to, but if I had more time I think I should learn a lot from discussing with him" (Misak, p. 349). In fact, Ramsey was instrumental in Wittgenstein getting his PhD at Cambridge, using the *Tractatus* as his thesis.

14. Richard Burian has suggested that Wittgenstein may be referring to Beethoven's *Große Fuge* (Great Fugue), originally intended as the last movement of the string quartet no. 13, op. 130. Critics and audiences hated the piece (which was longer than all five of the other movements in the quartet), so the publisher more or less forced Beethoven to substitute a rather innocuous last movement into the quartet before he would risk publishing it.

15. Wittgenstein's attitude towards Sigmund Freud (1856–1939) was very critical, but he nevertheless took notice of much in Freud's writing, for example, the notion that in some sense one is saying something in one's dreams. Before 1914, Wittgenstein's interest in psychology was limited to his experiments on rhythm, but in his 1942 to 1946 discussions with Rush Rhees, he considered himself a student and follower of Freud. On the other hand, Wittgenstein considered harmful the enormous influence of psychoanalysis in Europe and the United States. See Wittgenstein, *Lectures and Conversations*, pp. 41–52; and also Wittgenstein's 1945 letter to Norman Malcolm in Malcolm's *Memoir*, pp. 100f. [I.S.]

16. This sentence was written in English.

occurred to me. But then I must tell myself that it's quite impossible that one will ever occur to me, because for that I am missing something essential or <u>the</u> essential. That is why I am thinking of it as such a high ideal because I could then in a way sum up my life; and set it down crystallized. And even if it were but a small, shabby crystal, yet a crystal.

29.[4.30]

I feel well only when I am in a certain sense enthusiastic. Then again I fear the collapse of this enthusiasm.

Today Mrs. Moore[17] showed me a stupid review of a performance of Bruckner's 4th symphony where the reviewer complains about Bruckner & also talks disrespectfully of Brahms & Wagner.[18] At first it didn't make an impression on me since it is natural that everything—great & small—is barked at by dogs. Then it pained me after all. In a certain sense I feel touched (strangely) when I think that the mind is never understood.

30.[4.30]

Unproductive & sluggish. On yesterday's matter:[19] It always makes me think: did these great ones suffer so unspeakably so that some buttface[20] can come today & deliver his opinion about them. This thought often fills me with a sort of hopelessness.—Yesterday I sat for a while in the garden of Trinity[21] & there I thought, strange how

17. Dorothy Mildred Moore, née Ely (1892–1977) attended Newnham College from 1912 to 1915, and in 1915, the lectures of G. E. Moore, whom she married on November 11, 1915. [I.S.]

18. Anton Bruckner's (1824–1896) fourth symphony in E-flat major is also called the "romantic" symphony. *Culture and Value* contains various remarks by Wittgenstein on Bruckner, including one from 1934 or 1937 where Bruckner is discussed in relation to Wagner and Brahms: "In the days of silent film all the classics were played with the films, but not Brahms & Wagner. Not Brahms, because he is too abstract. I can imagine an exciting scene in a film accompanied by Beethoven's or Schubert's music and might gain some sort of understanding of the music from the film. But not an understanding of music by Brahms. Bruckner on the other hand does go with a film" (p. 25/29). [I.S.]

19. The German word is nearly illegible and might be deciphered "*gestrigen* (yesterday's matter)" or "*geistigen* (the matter of the mind or spirit)."

20. Wittgenstein wrote "*arschgesicht.*"

21. On June 19, 1929, Wittgenstein had received a stipend from Trinity College for the continuation of his research. While a student before World War I, after his appointment later in the year (on December 12, 1930) to a five-year term as Research Fellow, and again in 1939 as professor of philosophy, he lived in the same rooms on Whewell's Court in Cambridge's Trinity College. [I.S.]

the well developed physique of all these people goes together with complete unspiritedness (I don't mean lack of intellect.).[22] And how on the other hand a theme by Brahms is full of vigor, grace, & drive & he himself had a potbelly. In contrast the spirit of our contemporaries has no springs under its feet.

All day I want nothing but eat & sleep. It is as if my spirit were tired. But from what? In all these days I haven't really worked at all. Feel dumb & cowardly.

1.5.[30]

It takes extraordinarily long until something is clear to me.—This is true in various spheres. My relation to others, for example, always becomes clear to me only after a long time. It is as if it took colossally long for the large patch of fog to recede & the object itself to become visible. But during this time I am not even quite clearly aware of my unclarity. And all of a sudden I then see how the matter really is or was. And probably that's why I am useless whenever reasonably quick decisions need to be made. I am so to speak blinded for a while & only then the scales fall from my eyes.[23]

2.5.[30]

In my lectures[24] I often seek to gain favor with my audience through a somewhat comic turn; to entertain them so that they willingly hear me out. That is certainly something bad.

I am often pained by the thought of how much the success or value of what I do depends on how I am disposed. More so than for a concert-singer. Nothing is as it were stored up in me; nearly everything must be produced at the moment. That—I believe—is a very unusual sort of activity or life.

---

22. Wittgenstein contrasts *"geistlosigkeit* (mindlessness, unspiritedness)" and *"verstandlosigkeit* (lack of intellect)." In this and the following sentences, *"geist"* is, therefore, translated "spirit" and not "mind."

23. This colloquial German idiom derives from the story of Saul's conversion in Acts 9:18.

24. On January 20, 1930 (the day after Ramsey's death), Wittgenstein embarked upon his very first course of lectures by invitation of Richard Braithwaite on behalf of the Moral Science Faculty. "Braithwaite asked him under what title the course should be announced. After a long silence Wittgenstein replied: 'The subject of the lectures would be philosophy. What else can be the title of the lectures but Philosophy'" (Monk, p. 289).

Since I am very weak, I am extremely dependent upon the opinion of others.[25] At least at the moment of action. Except when I have a long time to collect myself.

A good word from someone or a friendly smile has a lasting effect on me, pleasantly encouraging & assuring, & an unpleasant, that is, unfriendly word has an equally long effect, depressing.

Being alone then in my room provides the greatest relief, there I restore my equilibrium. At least a mental equilibrium even though my nerves retain the impression.

The best state for me is the state of enthusiasm because it consumes the ridiculous thoughts at least partially & renders them harmless.

Everything or nearly everything I do, these entries included, is tinted by vanity & the best I can do is as it were to separate, to isolate the vanity & do what's right in spite of it, even though it is always watching. I cannot chase it away. Only sometimes it is not present.[26]

I love Marguerite very much & am very anxious that she might not be healthy since I haven't gotten a letter from her in more than a week. When I am alone I think of her again & again but at other times too. Were I more decent, my love for her would be more decent too. And yet I love her now as tenderly as I can. Tenderness is perhaps not what I am lacking. But decency.

6.5.[30]

Reading Spengler Decline[27] etc. & in spite of many irresponsibilities in the particulars, find <u>many</u> real, significant thoughts. Much, perhaps most of it, is completely in touch with what I have often thought myself. The possibility of a number of closed systems which, once one has them, look as if one is the continuation of another.

---

25. Compare a coded entry from the year 1929 in MS 107, p. 76: "What others think of me always occupies me to an extraordinary extent. I often aim to make a good impression. That is, I very frequently think about the impression I make on others and find it pleasant when I deem it good and otherwise unpleasant" (*Wiener Ausgabe*, vol. 2, p. 45). [I.S.]

26. See also Wittgenstein's coded reflections on his vanity in 1929 in MS 107, pp. 74–76 (*Wiener Ausgabe*, vol. 2, pp. 44–45).

27. Spengler, *The Decline of the West*, first published 1918–1922. Along with Boltzmann, Hertz, Schopenhauer, Frege, Russell, Kraus, Loos, Weininger, and Sraffa, Wittgenstein considered Spengler (1880–1936) one of those who influenced him (*Culture and Value*, p. 14/16, see also p. 19/21). See also Monk, pp. 299–303. [I.S.]

And all this has to do with the thought that we do not know (consider) how much can be taken away from—or given to—the human being.

The other day I happened to read in Buddenbrooks of typhoid & how Hanno B. in his final illness no longer recognized anyone except a friend.[28] And there it struck me that one generally considers this self-evident, thinking, of course, this is only natural once the brain is so deteriorated. But while in reality it is not ordinarily the case that we see people & not <u>recognize</u> them, what we call "recognizing" is only a special capacity which we could easily lose without being regarded inferior. I mean: It seems self-evident to us that we "recognize" people & it seems total deterioration when someone does not recognize them. But this brick can very well be missing from the building & not a hint of deterioration.[29] (This thought is again closely related to those of Freud, to the one on slips.)

That is, we consider all we <u>have</u> as self-evident & do not even know that we could be complete even without this & that, which we don't even recognize as some special capacity since to us it seems to belong to the completeness of our intellect.

It's a shame that Spengler did not stick with his Good Thoughts & went further than what he can answer for. Greater cleanliness, however, would have made his thought more difficult to understand, but only this would really have made it lastingly effective, too.[30] Thus is the thought that the string instruments assumed their <u>Definitive</u> Shape between 1500 and 1600 of <u>enormous</u> magnitude (& symbolism).[31] Only most people see nothing in such a thought if one gives it to them without much ado. It is as if someone believed that a human being keeps on developing without limit & one told him: look, the cranial sutures of a child close at . . . years & that

---

28. Thomas Mann's novel *Buddenbrooks* appeared in 1901. Its penultimate chapter objectively describes the course of typhoid and only implies the death of Hanno Buddenbrook. Hanno belongs to the third generation of a merchant's family in which a growth of sensitivity and awareness comes at the cost of diminished vitality and social position. Hanno embodies tender fragility and aesthetic sensibility. His detachment from the life of the bourgeoisie becomes complete through his musical inclinations. [I.S.]

29. An actual case very much like this is described and discussed by Oliver Sacks in the title essay in his collection *The Man Who Mistook His Wife for a Hat*.

30. Wittgenstein frequently invokes the goal of "*reinheit*" or purity. Here he considers Spengler's "*reinlichkeit*," which designates hygiene, neatness, cleanliness.

31. See Spengler, vol. 1, chapter 1, "The Meaning of Numbers," section 4 (p. 62): "The string instruments assumed their definitive shape 1480–1530 in Northern Italy."

shows already that development comes everywhere to an end, that what is developing here is a self-contained whole which at some point will be completely present & not a sausage which can run on indefinitely.

16 years ago when I had the thought that the law of causality is insignificant in itself & that there is a way of regarding the world which does not bear it in mind, I felt the beginning of a New Era.[32]

In one regard I must be a very modern person since the cinema has such an extraordinarily beneficial effect on me. I cannot imagine any rest for the mind more adequate to me than an American movie. What I see & the music give me a blissful sensation perhaps in an infantile way but therefore of course no less powerful. In general as I have often thought & said a film is something very similar to a dream & the thoughts of Freud are directly applicable to it.

A discovery is neither great nor small; it depends on what it signifies to us.

We view the Copernican discovery as something great—because we know that it <u>signified</u> something great in its time & perhaps because a resonance of this significance comes across to us—& now we infer by analogy that Einstein's discoveries etc. are something at least equally great. But they are—no matter how great their practical value, many-sided interest etc.—only as <u>great</u> as they are <u>significant</u> (symbolic).[33] It is with this of course as it is—for example—with heroism. A feat of weaponry of former times is—rightfully—praised as a feat of heroism. But it is quite possible that an equally or even more difficult feat of weaponry is today purely a matter of sport and is unjustly called a feat of heroism.[34] The difficulty, the practical significance, all that can be judged, as it were, from outside; the <u>greatness</u> of the heroism is determined by the <u>significance</u> of the action. By the pathos which is associated with the way of acting.

---

32. See 5.136, 6.32, 6.36 and 6.362 of the *Tractatus Logico-Philosophicus*: "If there were a law of causality, it might go: 'There are laws of nature.' But of course one can't say that: it shows itself.—What can be described that can also happen, and what is supposed to be excluded by the law of causality, that can't be described either." See also the entries of March 29 and October 15, 1915, in his *Notebooks 1914–1916*, pp. 41 and 84. Nothing seems to perfectly match this reference to "16 years ago."

33. Compare a remark from November 22, 1931: "The real achievement of a Copernicus or Darwin was not the discovery of a true theory but of a fertile new point of view (Aspekt)." (*Culture and Value*, p. 18/26). [I.S.]

34. Cf. Kierkegaard's parable "The Jewel on Thin Ice."

Because, however, a particular period of time, a particular race associates its pathos with very particular ways of acting, people are led astray & believe that the greatness, significance lies necessarily in that way of acting. And this belief is always reduced to absurdity just when a transvaluation of values[35] comes about through an upheaval, that is, when true pathos now settles upon another way of acting. Then—probably always—the old, now worthless bills remain in circulation for some time & people who are not quite honest pass them off as great & significant until one finds the new insight once again trivial & says "of course these old bills are worthless."

Drinking, at one time it is symbolic, at another boozing.

That is, the nimbus, or the genuine nimbus does not attach to the external fact, that is, not to the fact.

When teaching philosophy one can often say: "Scoundrels themselves who turn us into rogues!"[36]

8.[5.30]

I never committed a prank & probably won't ever commit one. It would not accord with my nature. (As with everything natural, I consider that neither a fault nor a merit.)

9.[5.30]

I am very much in love with R.,[37] have been for a long time of course, but it is especially strong now. And yet I know that the matter is in all probability hopeless. That is, I must be braced that she might get engaged & married any moment. And I know that this will be very painful for me. I therefore know that I should not hang my whole weight on this one rope since I know that eventually it will give. That is, I should remain standing with both feet on firm ground & only hold the rope but not hang on it. But that is difficult. It is difficult to love so unselfishly that one holds on to love & does not want to be held by it.—It is difficult to hold on to love in such a way that, when things go wrong one does not have to consider it a lost game but can say: I was prepared for that & this is also alright. One

---

35. Wittgenstein here uses a phrase that had assumed the status of a slogan with Nietzschean overtones (*"Umwertung aller Werte"*). See a related comment on October 22, 1930; p. 36, *infra*.

36. Wittgenstein here quotes from Friedrich Schiller's (1759–1805) play *Die Piccolimini* (the middle part of the *Wallenstein* trilogy), act 4, scene 7: *"Spitzbuben selbst, die uns zu Schelmen machen!"*

37. "R." stands for Marguerite's last name, Respinger.

could say "if you never sit on the horse and thus entrust yourself to it completely, then of course you can never be thrown but also never hope ever to ride." And all one can say to that is: You must wholly dedicate yourself to the horse & yet be braced that you may be thrown at any time.

One often thinks—and I myself <u>often</u> make this mistake—that everything one thinks can be written down. In reality one can only write down—that is, without doing something stupid & inappropriate—what arises in us in the form of writing. Everything else seems comical & as it were like dirt. That is, something that needs to be wiped off.

Vischer said "speaking is not writing" and thinking even less so.[38]

(I am always glad when I can start a new page.)

I think: Will I ever be able to hold R. in my arms again & kiss her? And this too I must be braced for & be able to reconcile myself that it will not happen.

Style is the expression of a general human necessity.[39] This holds for a writing style or a building style (and any other).

Style is general necessity viewed sub specie aeterni.[40]

Gretl once made a very good remark about Clara Schumann:[41] we were speaking about how she must have lacked—as it appears

---

38. Though the source of this quote could not be determined, Wittgenstein is most likely attributing it to Friedrich Theodor von Vischer (1807–1887). This German writer and philosopher is best known for his *Aesthetics or Science of the Beautiful*, for a work on *The Sublime and the Comical*, and for his parody *Faust: The Tragedy's Third Part*. [I.S.] The quoted statement "*Eine Rede ist keine Schreibe*" wittily reflects on the difference between speaking and writing. The noun "*Rede*" means "speech" but can also be taken as a substantivized form of the verb "*reden*" (as in "*ich rede*" or "I speak"). Vischer's statement now submits the verb "*schreiben*" (to write) to the same treatment which yields the crude noun "*Schreibe*"—a kind of slang. Wittgenstein takes this a step further by inventing yet another noun when he introduces "*eine Denke*" as derived from "*denken*" (to think). The strangeness of this play on words would be captured by translating as follows: "Vischer said 'a speech is no writ' and a think all the less so."

39. See Spengler, vol. 1, ch. VII, "Music and Plastic," section I, "The Arts of Form, Part 1" (p. 221): "Style is [. . .] a revelation of the metaphysical order, a mysterious 'must,' a destiny."

40. "Considered from the point of view of eternity." On various occasions, Wittgenstein used this expression from Spinoza's *Ethica* (1677), Book V, proposition 31, scholium. See remark 6.45 of the *Tractatus Logico-Philosophicus*; *Culture and Value*, p. 5/7; and an entry dated October 7, 1916. of his *Notebooks 1914–1916*, p. 83. [I.S.]

41. The third-oldest of Wittgenstein's sisters, Margarete Stonborough (1882–1958), married Jerome Stonborough in 1905. Gustav Klimt painted her wedding portrait. She was analyzed by Freud in 1937, and upon his departure from Vienna in 1938 fleeing the Nazi *Anschluss*, he inscribed a copy of *Future of an Illusion* with "Mrs. Margaret

to us—something human, about her prudishness etc. That's when Gretl said: "after all she was not what Ebner Eschenbach was" and that says it all.[42]

Loos, Spengler, Freud & I all belong to the same class that is characteristic for this age.[43]

12.[5.30]

Before my lectures I am always anxious even though so far it has always gone quite well. This anxiety then possesses me like a disease. It is by the way nothing other than test anxiety.

The lecture was mediocre. I am tired already, after all. None of my students has any idea how my brain must work in order to achieve what it achieves. If my achievement is not first rate, it is still the utmost of what I can achieve.[44]

16.[5.30]

I think that today it requires heroism to see things <u>not</u> as symbols in the sense of Kraus.[45] That is, to free oneself of a symbolism which can become routine. That is of course not to try seeing them as shallow again but to vaporize the clouds of the so-to-speak cheap

---

Stonborough on the occasion of my temporary departure." He never returned. Pianist and composer Clara Schumann, née Wieck (1819–1896) married Robert Schumann in 1840, was a close friend of Brahms, and had frequent contact with the Wittgenstein family. [I.S.]

42. The short stories, novels, and aphorisms of the Austrian writer Marie von Ebner-Eschenbach (1830–1916) testify to her human sympathy and social engagement. [I.S.] See Wittgenstein's diary entry for February 1, 1931, p. 39, *infra*, where he essentially repeats this remark.

43. Wittgenstein got to know Adolf Loos (1870–1933) in 1914. A pioneer of modernist architecture, Loos wrote in one of his critical pamphlets that "ornament is murder." In his memoir of Wittgenstein (*Letters from Ludwig Wittgenstein*, p. 127), Engelmann reports that Loos "once said to Wittgenstein: 'You are me!'"

44. Extensive dated notes of Wittgenstein's lectures were taken by G. E. Moore and published as *Wittgenstein: Lectures, Cambridge 1930–1933*, pp. 48–50.

45. This refers to the Austrian journalist, publicist, and writer Karl Kraus (1874–1936) who, from 1899 until his death, was editor of *Die Fackel*. Wittgenstein was an admirer of Kraus before World War I already and had *Die Fackel* forwarded to him during an extended stay in Norway from October 1913 until June 1914. Later on, Wittgenstein's attitude toward Kraus became increasingly critical. See, for example, his March 10, 1937, letter to Hänsel, in *Public and Private Occasions*, p. 301. Compare also a remark from January 11, 1948 (*Culture and Value*, p. 66/76): "Raisins may be the best part of a cake; but a sack of raisins is not better than a cake; & someone who is in a position to give us a sack of raisins still cannot bake a cake with them, let alone do something better. I am thinking of Kraus & his aphorisms, but also of myself & my philosophical remarks. A cake, that is not as it were: diluted raisins." [I.S.]

symbolism in a higher sphere (so that the air becomes transparent again).

It is difficult not to give in to this symbolism today.

Aside from the good & genuine, my book the *Tractatus Log.-Phil.* also contains kitsch, that is passages with which I filled in the gaps and so-to-speak in my own style. How much of the book consists of such passages I don't know & it is difficult to fairly evaluate now.

26.5.[30]
A man with more talent than I is awake then, when I sleep. And I sleep a lot and therefore it is easy to have more talent than I.

On May 16, Wittgenstein was awarded a lectureship commencing in October, and in June, his fellowship was extended, based on the report from Russell. Nearly five months and a summer in Austria have passed since the last entry; compare Monk's biography, pp. 298–304. Wittgenstein's classes were to begin on October 13.

2.10.[30]
Arrived in Cambridge. Left Vienna on the 26th & to Aunt Clara in Thumersbach & even if it was not as purely wonderful there with her as it usually is in Laxenburg, it was nice nevertheless & I parted with good feelings.[46] On the evening of the 27th I arrived in Gottlieben[47] & at first it was tense there since so much murkiness was in the air, & in the car in which she [Marguerite] picked me up & at dinner we sat quietly or talking of incidental things.[48] And spoke falteringly or forcedly fluent as one does when really heavy matters are pressing inside. After the evening meal I started talking about her last letter. I said that I noticed in it as not right a certain tone of triumph. That she wouldn't have written in a triumphant tone if everything was alright because then she would have seen the difficulties, too & accepted

---

46. Clara Wittgenstein (1850–1935) was an unmarried sister of Wittgenstein's father, Karl. For most of the year, she lived in the Wittgensteins' castle Laxenburg near Vienna. Karl's children had fond memories of the many holidays they spent with her. Thumersbach is a village in the province of Salzburg. [I.S.]

47. Gottlieben is a small town in Switzerland on the Rhine river just downstream from Lake Constance, very close to Germany and the city of Constance.

48. According to the original German, "*so viel unaufgeklärtes*" was in the air, which literally means so much that is "unenlightened," "unsettled," or "unresolved."

what is pleasant as a grace of heaven. I asked her to come to Vienna as soon as possible & work there. Only when we (especially I) had already talked quite a bit did I see that she was very unhappy. The thought of marriage was basically on her mind. To her that seemed to be the only real solution, after all. That's what she said she needs & nothing else. I asked her to be patient. that she will find what's right for her—appropriate to her. Most of all she should just work decently again & wait for the rest. Only with decent work everything would become clearer & more easily bearable for her.—During this conversation she was again rather distant toward me, tended to dodge my kisses & often had a virtually gloomy expression & looked away, which I had never seen in her & which as it were shocked me. She seemed cold toward me, bitter, & unhappy & almost dismissive. The next morning it was a little better. We went for a walk & chatted some & she was more accessible & affectionate. She was now decidedly in favor of going to Vienna & generally seemed calmer. But in the evening after another serious conversation she began to cry. I held her in my arms & she cried on my shoulder. But it was a good crying & she was softer afterwards & somewhat relieved. The next morning I decided to stay another day against my original plan. I had the feeling that it would be good for her (& in general). She too was—I think—glad about it. In the afternoon we went to Constance to mail a packet with two sweaters which she had knitted for Talla.[49] I had to stifle a certain jealousy or at least a similar feeling. Was it because of that or perhaps a reaction to the earlier excitement (for everything was incredibly strenuous for me) I felt vivid displeasure on the way home & I constantly choked up. I asked M. to walk ahead & followed later. It relieved me that I could be alone. At home I still had a pounding

---

49. Marguerite Respinger married Talla Sjögren (1902–1945) on New Year's Eve 1933. In a letter to Ilse Somavilla, dated September 25, 1995, she writes that she found in Talla a partner "who agreed with her way of life and signified peace." Talla was one of three sons of Carl and Mima Sjögren and the brother of Wittgenstein's friend Arvid. Along with Marguerite, he also belonged to Thomas Stonborough's circle of friends (all of whom ten to fifteen years younger than Wittgenstein). After his father's early death, Talla lived with his mother and brothers in Vienna, where he studied forestry and civil engineering. He acquired a farm in Chile, where he moved with Marguerite. There, he was shot and killed by a poacher in 1945. After his death, Marguerite married Benoît de Chambrier in 1949 and, from 1952, lived on an estate near Neuchâtel. In 1978, she wrote her privately published memoirs for family and friends *"Granny et son temps."* There is an extensive interview with Marguerite, including excerpts from her memoir, by Josef G. F. Rothhaupt and Aidan Seery, *"Ludwig Wittgenstein war ein 'Stern' in meinem Leben."* Madame de Chambrier lived in Geneva from 1982 until her death. [I.S.]

heart & retreated to my room where I felt somewhat wretched. Then, still excited, I joined M. in the parlor where we usually sat together. She was somewhat shocked (anxious) about my condition but it soon got better perhaps in part because I felt her sympathy. That evening our relationship was as good & tender as in earlier days & we kissed each other <u>for a long time</u> & I was glad to have stayed. But on the next day a letter from Talla arrived & this produced an upheaval, or setback in the mood. In the afternoon I rowed her to a small island on the Rhine where lots of reeds are growing as they do all around there & rowed into the reeds which I love doing very much. And there we sat in the boat & talked for a long time about our relationship. She said how little I mean to her when I am absent. And that she does not comprehend her relationship to me at all. That for example she lets herself be kissed by me & kisses me, of which she would shy away with everyone else, & doesn't understand why she can do it with me. I explained some things to her as well as I could. We drove to Basel together where she had something to do & waited with me at the train station for my train to Boulogne. During this trip to Basel, however, her mood grew worse and worse. She became gloomy again & sad. Whether due to the content of Talla's letter or only because it had arrived at all & reminded her of her futile wishes, I don't know. I held her hand the whole time & spoke to her from time to time only to give her—though unconsciously—some small support. At the final farewell we kissed but I departed with a heavy heart & with the feeling of leaving her not in a good state. I arrived in London yesterday afternoon & drove right away to Murakami[50] whose good & affectionate manner helped me. I then spent the evening with Gilbert[51] & we were actually quite merry even though my heavy feeling never left me as is natural. This morning I wrote a long letter to Gretl in which I described as well as I could the result of my stay with M. & the stay itself.[52] Then on to Cambridge where I am

---

50. According to a letter by Hermine Wittgenstein to Ludwig, probably from October 1932, Murakami was a London dealer of Japanese art; see *Wittgenstein's Family Letters*, p. 187. [I.S.]

51. Gilbert Pattisson (1908–1994) met Wittgenstein on a train when both returned in 1929 from Vienna to Cambridge. Pattison had traveled Europe extensively, became seriously ill with polio in 1927, and, in 1928, joined Emmanuel College in Cambridge to study foreign languages. Wittgenstein and he remained close friends throughout the 1930s, with Pattison spending many weekends in Cambridge. [I.S.]

52. This letter is not extant.

staying with Lettice who is very friendly & good to me.[53] I told her about Marguerite & our difficulties.—I am very unclear about the significance of all my experiences with M. I don't know where this is to lead, or what I should do to influence it in the best way and my egoism, too, interferes with my thoughts & perhaps does the most to confuse everything, even though I don't see this clearly.

3.[10.30]

Wrote to M. I am holding her hand—in my thoughts—as I did on the ride to Basel, even though I knew that she wasn't thinking of me, only so that she unconsciously has some support or help. Or so that she might remember it some day with good feelings.

4.[10.30]

Am saddened by the thought of not being able to help M. I am very weak & moody. If I remain strong, with the help of God,[54] I can perhaps help her through that.—It is possible that what she needs most of all is a strong & firm post that remains standing no matter how she flutters. Whether I will have the strength for that? And the necessary loyalty? May God grant me what is necessary.

I shouldn't be surprised if the music of the future were in unison. Or is that only because I cannot clearly imagine several voices? Anyway I can't imagine that the old <u>large</u> forms (string quartet, symphony, oratory etc.) will be able to play any role at all. If something comes it will have to be—I think—simple, <u>transparent</u>.

In a certain sense, naked.

Or will that hold only for a certain race, only for <u>one</u> kind of music(?)

7.10.[30]

Looking for an apartment & feeling miserable & restless. Incapable of collecting myself. Have not received a letter from M. & that too

---

53. After attending Newnham College in Cambridge, Lettice Cautley Ramsey, née Baker (1898–1985) received her MA in 1925 and, in the same year, married Frank Plumpton Ramsey (see footnote 10, *supra*). Lettice was a well-known photographer and, in 1932, became manager of the "Cambridge photographers" Ramsey and Muspratt. She was one of the few women in whose company Wittgenstein felt comfortable. When he returned to England early in 1929, he spent the first two weeks with Lettice and F. P. Ramsey in Cambridge. [I.S.] See Misak's biography of Ramsey (p. 347) for more about Lettice and Wittgenstein.

54. The diary contains only the abbreviated expression "d G.H." The editor [I.S.] conjectures that this stands for "*durch Gottes Hilfe*"—"with the help of God."

worries me. Terrible that there is no possibility of helping her or that at any rate I don't know how she can be helped. I don't know what word from me would do her good or whether it would be best for her to hear nothing from me. Which word won't she misunderstand? Which will she heed? One can almost always answer both ways & must ultimately leave it to God.

I have occasionally thought about my strange relationship with Moore.[55] I respect him greatly & have a certain, not inconsiderable affection for him. He on the other hand? He esteems my intellect, my philosophical talent highly, that is, he believes that I am very clever but his affection toward me is probably <u>quite</u> inconsiderable. And I construct this more than I feel it, for he is friendly to me, as to everyone & if he is different in this regard with different people, then I don't notice this difference because I do not understand just this nuance. I am active or aggressive but he passive & therefore I don't notice in our dealings at all how much of a stranger I am to him. I remind myself in this regard of my sister Helene who is the same way with people.[56] This leads to the awkward situation that one feels as if one had imposed oneself upon people without wanting to or being aware of it. Suddenly it hits one that the relation to them is not as one assumed because they do not reciprocate the feelings one bears toward them; but one hadn't noticed it since the difference of roles in these interactions at any rate is so great that the nuances of like & dislike can easily hide behind them. I asked Moore today whether he is glad when I come to see him regularly (as in the previous year) & said that I will not be offended whatever the answer turns out to be. He said that it wasn't clear to himself, & I: he should think it over & inform me; which he promised to do. I said I could not promise that his answer will not sadden me, yet, however, that

---

55. George Edward Moore (1873–1958) was a professor in Cambridge from 1925 to 1939, guest professor in the United States from 1940 to 1944, and editor of the philosophical journal *Mind*. Wittgenstein attended Moore's lectures briefly in 1912. Moore visited Wittgenstein in Norway for two weeks in April 1914 where Wittgenstein dictated notes to Moore, later published in *Notebooks: 1914–1916*, Appendix II. Moore attended Wittgenstein's lectures from 1930 to 1933, and his notes are published as *Wittgenstein: Lectures, Cambridge 1930–1933*. More on Wittgenstein's relationship with Moore can be found in his March 10, 1937, letter to Hänsel, in *Public and Private Occasions*, p. 301. See also Malcolm's *Memoir*, p. 116. [I.S.]

56. Helene Salzer, née Wittgenstein (1879–1956) was Wittgenstein's second-oldest sister. She was called Lenka by her family. Ludwig especially appreciated her humor and musicality. [I.S.]

it will not offend me.—And I believe it is God's will with me, that I shall hear & <u>bear</u> it.

Again and again I believe that I am, or am supposed to be a sort of Peter Schlemihl[57] & if this name means as much as unlucky fellow, this signifies that through outward unhappiness he is supposed to become happy.

8.10.[30]

In the new apartment, it doesn't fit me yet, like a new suit.[58] I feel cold & uncomfortable. Writing this only to be writing something & to talk to myself. I could say: now I am finally alone with myself & must gradually get into conversation with me.

In the metropolitan civilization the spirit [*Geist*] can only huddle in some corner. And yet it is not for instance atavistic & superfluous but hovers above the ashes of culture as an (eternal) witness—as if an avenger of the deity.[59]

As if it were awaiting a new incarnation (in a new culture).

What would the great satirist of this time have to look like?

It is 3 weeks since I thought of philosophy but every thought of it is so foreign to me as if I had not thought such things for years anymore. In my first lecture I want to speak about the specific problems of philosophy & have the feeling: how can I say anything about this, I don't know them anymore.[60]

---

57. Adelbert von Chamisso (1781–1838) published "The Wonderful Story of Peter Schlemihl" in 1814. This is a fairy tale of a man without a shadow who learns to accommodate himself to his luckless lot. Compare Wittgenstein's remark about the story in *Culture and Value*, p. 14/21; also *Wiener Ausgabe*, vol. 4, p. 38. [I.S.]

58. It is difficult to determine where Wittgenstein lived at that time. From the list of addresses published by the *Cambridge University Reporter*, Wittgenstein's is missing for October 1930. The January 1931 edition lists "6, Grantchester Road" and, for April 1931, "C1 Bishop's Hostel, Trinity College." Since there was occasionally a delay in printing addresses, it cannot be ruled out that Wittgenstein lived at 6, Grantchester Road in October 1930 already. He probably rented two rooms in the house of George and Alison Quiggin. [I.S., based on information provided in a letter dated October 27, 1995, by Jonathan Smith, Trinity College Library]

59. See a remark from January 11, 1930, in *Culture and Value*, p. 3/5: "The earlier culture will become a heap of rubble & finally a heap of ashes; but spirits will hover over the ashes" (this remark has been published in context in *Wiener Ausgabe*, vol. 2, p. 166). [I.S.]

60. Wittgenstein began his lectures for the Michaelmas term on October 13 with the following remarks about the role and difficulties of philosophy: "The nimbus of philosophy has been lost. For now we have a method of doing philosophy. [. . .] What we are in fact doing is to tidy up our notions, to make clear what *can* be said about the world. [. . .] This activity of clearing up is philosophy. [. . .] The only way to do

9.[10.30]

Even though I am with quite friendly people (or just because of it?) I constantly feel disturbed—even though they do not actively disturb me—& cannot come to myself.[61] That's an awful state. Every word I hear them speak disturbs me. I feel surrounded & prevented from getting down to work.

In my room I feel not alone but exiled.

16.[10.30]

Feeling generally a little better. I cannot work for myself yet & that is in part due to the conflict in me of the English and German modes of expression. I can really work only when I can continuously converse with myself in German. But for my lectures I must now arrange things in English & so I am disturbed in my German thought; at least until a peaceful accord has formed between the two & that takes some time, perhaps very long.

I am capable of accommodating myself to all situations. When I come into new living quarters under new circumstances I undertake as soon as possible to devise a technique to endure the various discomforts & to avoid friction: I accommodate myself to the given circumstances. And thus I accommodate myself gradually also with thinking, only this cannot be done simply through a certain degree of self-mastery & intellect. Instead this must form & arrange itself on its own. Just as one finally does fall asleep in this strained position. And being able to work is in so many ways similar to being able to fall asleep. If one thinks of Freud's definition of sleep one could say that both cases concern a shift of the troops of interest.[62] (In the one

---

philosophy is to do everything twice" (Lee, *Wittgenstein's Lectures 1930–1932*, pp. 21–24). And also Moore's notes in *Wittgenstein: Lectures, Cambridge 1930–1933*, pp. 67–68. [I.S.]

61. "*zu mir kommen*" in the sense of regaining consciousness as when someone "comes to."

62. In the fifth lecture of his *General Introduction to Psychoanalysis*, Freud addresses the question of what sleep is: "That is a physiological or biological problem concerning which much is still in dispute. We can come to no decisive answer, but I think we may attempt to define one psychological characteristic of sleep. Sleep is a condition in which I refuse to have anything to do with the outer world, and have withdrawn my interest from it [*mein Interesse von ihr abgezogen habe*]. I go to sleep by retreating [*zurückziehen*] from the outside world and warding off the stimuli proceeding from it. Again, when I am tired from that world I go to sleep. I say to it as I fall asleep: 'Leave me in peace, for I want to sleep.' The child says just the opposite: 'I won't go to sleep yet; I am not tired, I want more things to happen to me.' Thus the biological object

case it is merely a withdrawal, in the other a withdrawal and con-centration at some location.)

Moore later answered my question to the effect that while he does not actually like me, my company nevertheless does him so much good that he thinks he should continue to keep it. That is a peculiar case.

I am on the whole more respected than loved. (And the former of course not justly) while there would be some reason to like me.

I believe that my mental apparatus is built in an extraordinarily complicated & delicate manner & therefore more sensitive than nor-mal.[63] Much that wouldn't disturb a cruder mechanism disturbs it, puts it out of action. Just as a particle of dust can bring a fine instru-ment to a standstill but will not influence a cruder one.

It is curious, strange, how happy it makes me to be able to write something about logic again even though my remark is not particu-larly inspired. But merely being able to be alone with it gives me that feeling of happiness. The capacity to be sheltered again, at home again, in the warmth again, that is what my heart yearns for & what does it such good.

18.[10.30]

The manner in writing is a sort of mask behind which the heart makes faces as it pleases.

Genuine modesty is a religious matter.[64]

19.[10.30]

When talking with people who don't really understand one, one al-ways feels that one has made a fool of oneself, at least I do. And here this happens to me again and again. One has the choice between remaining a <u>complete</u> stranger & this unpleasant experience. And of course I could say: Here too, I have this or that person, after all, with whom I can talk without danger of this; & why don't I withdraw altogether from the others? But that's difficult & unnatural for me.

---

of sleep seems to be recuperation, its psychological characteristic the suspension of interest in the world" (p. 92, compare also p. 424). [I.S.]

63. Wittgenstein's sister Hermine compared him to a sensitive "precision instru-ment" in her memoir in *Recollections of Wittgenstein*, p. 4.

64. Compare a remark from roughly 1944 in *Culture and Value*, p. 45/51: "People are religious to the extent that they believe themselves to be not so much *imperfect* as *sick*. People who are halfway decent will believe themselves utterly imperfect, but religious people believe themselves *wretched*." [I.S.]

The difficulty is how to speak in a friendly way with someone & not touch upon points on which we cannot understand each other. To speak seriously & so that one does not touch upon anything inessential which must lead to misunderstandings. This is just about impossible for me.

22.[10.30]

Our age is really an age of the transvaluation of all values. (The procession of humanity turns a corner & what used to be the way up is now the way down etc.) Did Nietzsche have in mind what is now happening & does his achievement consist in anticipating it & finding a word for it?[65]

In art, too, there are people who believe that they can forcibly bring about their eternal life by doing good works & those who cast themselves in the arms of grace.[66]

When something is wrong with me like today's sore throat I get very anxious right away, think, what'll happen if it gets worse & I need a doctor & the doctors here are worthless & perhaps I must cancel my lectures for a long time etc.—as if the Good Lord had made a contract with me that here he will leave me undisturbed. When I see such anxiety in others, I say "that must simply be endured"; but it is very difficult for me to adjust myself to endurance rather than enjoyment.

One likes to see the hero in the other as a drama (that is performed for us) but to be even the least bit of a hero oneself leaves a different taste.

In a translucent light heroism has a different color than in a conspicuous one. (bad)

The difference is more like that between a dish that is seen & one that is eaten. Because here the experience is really an entirely different one.

1.11[.30]

What disturbs me in my sleep also disturbs me in my work. Whistling & speaking but not the sound of machines or at least <u>much</u> less.

---

65. "Transvaluation of values! [*Umwertung der Werte*]" is the concluding sentence of Nietzsche's *The Antichrist* (p. 656). He later conceived a larger work with the title *Transvaluation of All Values.*

66. Presumably an allusion to Romans 11:6 and 2 Timothy 1:9.

9.[11.30]

Patriotism is love of an idea.

16.[11.30]

Sleep & mental work correspond to one another in many respects. Apparently in that both involve a withdrawal of attention from certain things.

26.[11.30]

A being that stands in contact with God is strong.

> Almost two months have lapsed since the previous entry. Again, Wittgenstein has just recently returned to Cambridge from a vacation in Austria. Classes for the Lent term would begin for Wittgenstein on January 19.

1931

16.1.31

There is a tendency in my life to base this life on the fact that I am much cleverer than the others. But when this assumption threatens to break down, when I see by how much less clever I am than other people, only then do I become aware how wrong this foundation is in general even if the assumption is or were right. When I tell myself: first I must imagine that all other people are just as clever as I am—by which as it were I forgo the advantage of birth, the inherited riches—and then let's see how far I get through goodness alone, when I tell myself that, I become aware of my smallness.

Or shall I say it so: How much of what I tend to take for the stamp of character in me is only the result of a shabby talent!

It is almost similar to looking at the medals of valor on one's uniform[67] & saying to oneself: "I am quite a fellow." Until one notices

---

67. Monk's biography has this to say about Wittgenstein's own medal of valor, which he received after the Austrian offensive of June 15, 1918: "Once again he was cited for his bravery: 'His exceptionally courageous behaviour, calmness, sang-froid, and heroism,' ran the report, 'won the total admiration of the troops.' He was recommended for the Gold Medal for Valour [. . .] but was awarded instead the Band of the Military Service Medal with Swords, it being decided that his action, though brave, had been insufficiently consequential to merit the top honor" (p. 154). See also

the same medals on many people & must tell oneself that they are not at all the reward for bravery but the recognition of a particular skill. Again and again, where I would like to have a sense of myself as a master, I feel like a schoolboy. Like a schoolboy who thought he knew a lot & discovers that in relation to others he knows nothing.

Saturday 17.[1.31]

I find it difficult to work, that is to prepare my lecture—even though it is high time—because my thoughts are with my relationship to Marguerite. A relationship in which I can draw satisfaction just about only from what I give. I must ask God that he lets me work.

27.[1.31]

The music of past times always corresponds to certain maxims of the good & right at that time. Thus we recognize in Brahms the principles of Keller etc etc.[68] And that is why good music which was found today or recently, which is therefore modern, must seem absurd, for if it corresponds to any of the maxims articulated today it must be dirt. This sentence is not easy to understand but it is so: Today no one is clever enough to formulate what is right & all formulas, maxims, which are articulated are nonsense. The truth would sound completely paradoxical to everyone. And the composer who feels it in him must stand with this feeling in opposition to everything that is nowadays articulated & according to present standards he must therefore appear absurd, stupid. But not engagingly absurd (for after all, this is basically what corresponds to the present attitude) but

---

McGuinness's description of Wittgenstein's medals in 1916 (*Wittgenstein: A Life*, pp. 242, 258, and 262–63).

68. The Swiss author Gottfried Keller (1819–1890) participated in the political struggles of the so-called regeneration. He forged close ties to Ludwig Feuerbach, whose worldview influenced him decisively. Keller's own style of poetic realism emerged from his encounter with late romanticism (see especially his novel *Green Henry* or the collection of novellas *The People of Seldwyla*). Paul Engelmann reports that Keller was one of the few great writers whom Wittgenstein "admired tenderly, even passionately." Keller was to have commanded a kind of "truthfulness" and the "complete appropriateness of expression to sensation" that Wittgenstein was looking for in art (p. 86f.). In his *Lectures and Conversations* (p. 41), Wittgenstein says that in Keller he found a "wisdom" which he "would never expect from Freud." [I.S.]

vacuous. Labor is an example of this where he created something really significant as in some few pieces.[69]

One could conceive a world where the religious people are distinguished from the irreligious ones only in that the former were walking with their gaze turned upwards while the others looked straight ahead. And here the upward gaze is really related to one of our religious gestures, but that is not essential & it could be the other way round with the religious people looking straight ahead etc. What I mean is that in this case religiosity would not seem to be expressed in words at all & these gestures would still say as much & as little as the words of our religious writings.

1.2.[31]

My sister Gretl once made an excellent remark about Clara Schumann. We were speaking about a trait of prudishness in her personality & that she was lacking something & Gretl said: "she does not have what Ebner Eschenbach has." And that sums it all up.[70]

Can one say: she was lacking genius—Labor once told me that in his presence she stated her doubt that a blind person could do this & that in music. I don't know anymore what it was. Labor was evidently outraged about this & told me "but he can so." And I thought: how characteristic with all the tact she must have had to make such a half pitying, half disparaging remark about a blind musician.—That is bad nineteenth century, Ebner Eschenbach would never have done this.

---

69. Josef Labor (1842–1924) was a Viennese composer who went blind at a young age and received his training at the Vienna Institute for the Blind and its Academy of Music. At his first piano recital in 1863 he found general recognition and was appointed royal chamber-pianist in Hannover. In 1866, he began learning in Vienna to also play the organ and started in 1879 to perform as an organ virtuoso. He was soon considered the best organist in Austria. His works include a violin concerto, a concert piece for piano and orchestra, chamber music and vocal compositions, and piano pieces. His students included Arnold Schönberg. An association was founded in 1923 to "facilitate the effectiveness of the organ virtuoso and musical artist Josef Labor" and "to enable the printing of numerous unpublished tone poems." Labor was a frequent visitor at the Wittgensteins' house and was sponsored especially by Hermine. McGuinness wrote that Labor's chamber music was the only contemporary music that passed muster with Wittgenstein (*Wittgenstein: A Life*, p. 125). [I.S.] For a more detailed account, see *Wittgenstein und die Musik*, especially Alber's essay on Josef Labor and music in the Wittgenstein family; and Szabados, *Wittgenstein as Philosophical Tone-Poet*.

70. Wittgenstein here repeats almost verbatim a remark from earlier; pp. 26–27, *supra*.

5.[2.31]

We are imprisoned in our skin.

7.[2.31]

I need an extraordinary amount of energy in order to hold my classes. I see this when I am lax in the slightest & right away incapable of preparing myself for the lecture.

The three variations before the entrance of the choir[71] in the 9th Symphony could be called the early spring of joy,[72] its spring and its summer.

If my name lives on then only as the Terminus ad quem of great occidental philosophy.[73] Somewhat like the name of the one who burnt down the library of Alexandria.[74]

8.[2.31]

I tend a bit to sentimentality. But please, no sentimental relations.— Not to language either.

It seems to me that nothing more than self-righteousness will forever diminish the remembrance of a person. Also when it appears in the guise of modesty.

With increasing age I am becoming more & more logically near-sighted.

My power of seeing how things go together is diminishing. And my thinking increasingly suffers from shortness of breath.

---

71. This probably refers to the reminiscences to the first three movements on the theme of joy. These occur in the second chaos-moment of the final movement, followed by the baritone solo (*"O Freunde, nicht diese Töne"*) and then the choir. (Communication from Friedrich Heller, Vienna.) [I.S.]

72. The German *"Vorfrühling"* literally means "pre-spring," the time when spring is just announcing itself.

73. *"Terminus ad quem"*: the endpoint or destination.—"great" was inserted into the line.

74. The library's 700,000 scrolls (including Aristotle's dialogues) were destroyed during the Alexandrian war in 47 BCE. [I.S.] Redpath recounts an incident in his *Memoir* (pp. 44–45): "In the early summer of 1936 I was having tea with Wittgenstein in his rooms in Whewell's Court, the day after some great party in the Court had been held. . . . There had been fireworks, and also some actual minor conflagration. . . . The porter said he hoped that Wittgenstein had not been disturbed by the party the night before. Wittgenstein said he thought the fireworks had been a good thing. This seemed to shock the porter, and he said that something had been set on fire. 'Good!' said Wittgenstein, which the porter clearly considered a somewhat eccentric comment, and accordingly rejoined that he was afraid they might damage the 'Ermes.' 'That's just what I hoped they would do!' was Wittgenstein's final riposte. He had long had the greatest contempt for that *objet d'art* . . ."

The task of philosophy is to soothe the mind about meaningless questions. Whoever doesn't tend to such questions doesn't need philosophy.[75]

9.[2.31]
My thoughts are so evanescent, evaporate so fast, like dreams which must be recorded immediately upon awakening if they are not to be forgotten right away.

10.[2.31]
The professor of mathematics Rothe once told me that Schumann lost a great part of his rightful influence through the effectiveness of Wagner.[76]—There is much truth in this thought.

13.[2.31]
Reading numbs my soul.
    Bread & games, but also games in the sense in which mathematics, yes even physics is a game. Their mind is always set on games in the arts, in the laboratory as well as on the soccer field.[77]

14.[2.31]
The stomach can be accustomed to little nourishment, but not the body; it suffers from malnutrition even when the stomach no longer objects, indeed, even when it would already reject more nourishment. Now this is similar to the expression of emotion: affection, gratitude etc. One can artificially curb these expressions until one shies away from what used to be natural but the rest of the spiritual organism suffers from malnutrition.

---

75. Cf. §133 in the *Philosophical Investigations*. [I.S.]

76. Wittgenstein is probably referring to Rudolf Rothe (1873–1942), professor at the Technical University of Berlin and in the 1920s author of a multi-volume popular textbook for physicists, mathematicians, and engineers (*Höhere Mathematik*, Leipzig: Teubner Verlag). [I.S.]

77. "*Brot und Spiel* [bread and games, bread and circuses]" translates the Latin phrase "*panem et circenses*" (what governments give the masses to keep them distracted and content). This sentence could also be translated as follows: "As on the soccer field, their spirit (that of mathematics and of physics) always goes for games in the arts, in the laboratory." Malcolm's *Memoir* (p. 55) relates that Wittgenstein told Freeman Dyson that a soccer match first prompted his thought that "in language we play *games* with *words*."

19.[2.31]
I know <u>every possible</u> slightest & greatest wretchedness because I myself committed it.

20.[2.31]
Most people pursue in their way of acting the path of least resistance; and so do I.

22.[2.31]
Hamann considers God a part of nature & at the same time like nature.[78]

And doesn't this express the religious paradox: "How can nature be a part of nature?"

It is curious: Moses Mendelssohn appears already in his letters to Hamann like a journalist.[79]

Dealing with authors like Hamann and Kierkegaard makes their editors presumptuous. The editor of the Cherubinic Wanderer would never feel this temptation, nor would the editor of Augustine's Confessions or of a work by Luther.[80]

It is probably that the <u>irony</u> of an author inclines the reader to become presumptuous.

It is then roughly like this: they say they know that they don't know anything but are enormously proud of this recognition.

I am not interested in a natural moral law; or at least no <u>more</u> than in any other law of nature & no more than in that which makes someone transgress the moral law. If the moral law is natural I am inclined to defend its transgressor.

---

78. Johann Georg Hamann (1730–1788) was a close associate of Jacobi, Kant, and Herder. He objected to the neglect by Enlightenment rationalism of the historical character of the human being. According to Hamann, reason cannot be separated from intuition, understanding, and historical experience: There is no thinking without language. On the parallels between Hamann's and Wittgenstein's philosophy, see Hans Rochelt's "Das Creditiv der Sprache." [I.S.]

79. The philosopher Moses Mendelssohn (1729–1786) identified Judaism with the Enlightenment religion of reason. Only one letter to Hamann is known (March 2, 1762), but Wittgenstein might have had in mind his letters on literature in which Mendelssohn writes critically about Hamann (see his *Gesammelte Schriften*, vol. 4, part 2, pp. 99–105, 403–12). [I.S.]

80. Angelus Silesius (1624–1677) published, under the title *Cherubinischer Wandersmann*, six volumes of pantheistic aphorisms on the relation between human beings, eternity, and God. [I.S.]

25.[2.31]

The idea that nowadays someone would convert from Catholicism to Protestantism or from Protestantism to Catholicism is embarrassing to me (as to many others). (In each of those cases in a different way.) Something that can (now) make sense only as a tradition is changed like a conviction. It is as if someone wanted to exchange the burial rites of our country for those of another.—Anyone converting from Protestantism to Catholicism appears like a mental monstrosity. No good Catholic priest would have done that, had he been born a non-Catholic. And the reverse conversion reveals abysmal stupidity.

Perhaps the former proves a deeper, the latter a more shallow stupidity.

1.3.[31]

Have reason to suppose now that Marguerite does not particularly care for me. And that is very strange for me. One voice in me says: Then it's over, & you must lose heart.—And another one says: That must not get you down, you had to anticipate it, & your life cannot be founded upon the occurrence of <u>some</u>, even if greatly desired case.

And the latter voice is right, but then this is the case of a human being who lives & is tormented by pain. He must struggle so that the pain does not spoil life for him. And then one is anxious about times of weakness.

This anxiety is of course only a weakness itself, or cowardice. For one always likes to rest, not having to fight. God be with her![81]

Someone who cannot finally entrust what he loves most into the hands of the gods but wants to keep tinkering with it himself, doesn't have the right love for it after all. For this is the severity which is supposed to be part of love. (I am thinking of the "Hermannsschlacht" & why Hermann wants to send only <u>one</u> messenger to his ally.[82])

---

81. Ilse Somavilla plausibly conjectures that "G.m.i.!" is short for "*Gott mit ihr!*"

82. Wittgenstein here refers to act 2, scene 10 of Heinrich von Kleist's (1777–1811) play *Die Hermannsschlacht*. The play deals with the victory of Arminius over the Romans in the year 9 AD. In the scene, Hermann wants to send Luitgar (along with his two sons) as his only messenger to Marbod. Luitgar asks permission to take two friends in case something happens to him. Hermann declines the request: "Who would want to thus tempt the powerful Gods?! Do you think the great work could be done without them? As if their lightning couldn't strike down three just as well

To forego certain precautions is not a <u>matter of convenience</u>, but what's least convenient in the world.

Beethoven is a realist through & through;[83] I mean his music is <u>totally</u> <u>true</u>, I want to say: he sees life <u>totally</u> as it is & then he exalts it. It is totally religion & not at all religious poetry. That's why he can console in real pain while the others fail & make one say to oneself: but this is not how it is. He doesn't lull one into a beautiful dream but redeems the world by viewing it like a hero, as it is.

Luther was no Protestant.

2.[3.31]

I am uncommonly cowardly, & I behave in life like a coward in battle.

7.[3.31]

Am fatigued from the work of the last months & quite beat from the torturous situation with Marguerite. Here I foresee a tragedy. And yet there is only one thing: to do one's best & keep working.

11.3.[31]

An excellent remark by Engelmann which often reoccurs to me:[84] During the construction when we were still working together he told me after a talk with the building contractor: "You can't talk logic with this man!"[85]—I: "I will teach him logic."—He: "And he will teach you psychology."

---

as one! You'll go alone; and if you arrive too late at Marbod's, or never, so be it! It is my fate to bear." [I.S.]

83. Compare Wittgenstein's remarks on Beethoven in the *Recollections of Wittgenstein*, by John King and by M. Drury, pp. 69f., 111f., and 115. [I.S.]

84. Paul Engelmann (1891–1965) studied architecture with Adolf Loos and served for a year as Karl Kraus's private secretary. In 1916, Wittgenstein took officers' training in Engelmann's hometown of Olmütz. Engelmann documents their friendship and the Olmütz discussion-circle in his *Memoir*. Working at first with Engelmann, Wittgenstein designed and built, from 1926 to 1928, a house for his sister, Margarete Stonborough, in Vienna's Kundmanngasse. [I.S.]

85. The contractor was probably Friedl. [I.S.] Compare *Culture and Value*, p. 15/22; and Hermine Wittgenstein's memoir in *Recollections of Wittgenstein*, pp. 6–8.

6.5.[31][86]

To be an apostle is a <u>life</u>. In part it surely expresses itself in what he says, but not in that it is true but in that he says it. Suffering for the idea defines him but here, too, it holds that the meaning of the sentence "this one is an apostle" lies in the mode of its verification. To describe an apostle is to describe a life. What impression this description makes on others must be left to them. Believing in an apostle means to relate toward him in such & such a way—relate actively.

If one does not want to get angry any more, one's joy too must change, it must not be the correlate to anger any longer.

On Kierkegaard:[87] I represent a life for you & now see how you relate to it, whether it tempts (urges) you to live like that as well, or what other relation to it you attain. Through this representation I would like to as it were loosen-up your life.

To what extent my thought takes flight, is of no concern (that is I don't know & don't ponder it). It has drive.—

"It is good because God commanded it" is the right expression for the lack of reason.[88]

An ethical proposition states "You shall do this!" or "That is good!" but not "These people say that this is good." But an ethical proposition is a personal act. Not a statement of fact.[89] Like an exclamation of admiration. Just consider that the justification of an "ethical proposition" merely attempts to refer the proposition back to others that make an impression on you. If in the end you don't

---

86. On March 10, 1931, Wittgenstein wrote to William Eccles: "I am going down for Easter vacation on Friday and coming up again about the 20th of April," in *Philosophical Occasions*, p. 9. By all indications, the following pages were all written on May 6, 1931.

87. Wittgenstein comments on one of the literary devices employed in the writings of the Danish philosopher Søren Kierkegaard (1813–1855).

88. See *Tractatus* 6.372 and also Waismann's notes of Wittgenstein (*Wittgenstein and the Vienna Circle*, p. 115): "According to the shallow interpretation the good is good because God wants it; according to the deeper interpretation God wants the good because it is good. I think the first conception is the deeper one: good is what God commands. For it cuts off any explanation as to 'why' it is good." [I.S.]

89. Compare *Tractatus* 6.422: "The first thought in setting up an ethical law of the form 'thou shalt . . .' is: And what if I do not do it? But it is clear that ethics has nothing to do with punishment and reward in the ordinary sense. This question as to the *consequences* of an action must therefore be irrelevant. At least these consequences will not be events. For there must be something right in the formulation of that question. There must be some sort of ethical reward and ethical punishment, but this must lie in the action itself. (And this is clear also that the reward must be something acceptable, and the punishment something unacceptable.)" [I.S.]

have disgust for this & admiration for that, then there is no justification worthy of that name.

Music composed at the piano, on the piano, music composed thinking with the quill & music composed exclusively by hearing within must bear a <u>completely</u> different character, & create a completely different sort of impression.

I definitely think that Bruckner composed by hearing within & by imagining the orchestra playing, that Brahms composed with the quill. Of course that presents matters much simpler than they are. Yet it hits upon <u>one</u> characteristic.[90]

The composer's writing of the notes should provide some insights about this. And indeed, Bruckner's writing was, I believe, clumsy & ponderous.

In Brahms the colors of the orchestral sound [are like] colors of trail-markers.

A tragedy could always, after all, begin with the words: "Nothing whatsoever would have happened, had not . . ."[91]

(Had not a corner of his clothing caught in the machine?)

But isn't that a one-sided view of tragedy which only lets it show that one encounter can determine our entire life?[92]

I think that there could be a theater today where one performs with masks. The characters would be just stylized human types. In the writings of Kraus this can be seen clearly. His plays could or should be performed in masks.[93] This corresponds, of course, to a

---

90. This is one of several remarks in these diaries that Wittgenstein copied into other manuscripts. In this case, a slight variant appears in MS 153a (1931) and can also be found in *Culture and Value* (p. 12/14): "Compositions composed at the piano, on the piano, those composed thinking with the quill & those composed exclusively by hearing within must be of a completely different kind, & make a completely different kind of impression. I definitely think that Bruckner composed only by hearing within & by imagining the orchestra playing, that Brahms composed with the quill. Of course that presents matters simpler than they are. Yet it hits upon <u>one</u> characteristic." [I.S.] There is clear evidence that Wittgenstein copied this *into* rather than *from* MS 153a: His copy in MS 153a originally formulated like the diary-version "must bear a <u>completely</u> different character" and changed this only then into "must be of a completely different kind."

91. This and the following three remarks Wittgenstein also copied almost verbatim into MS 153a. They are included in *Culture and Value*, p. 12/14.

92. Wittgenstein copied a version of this into MS 153a.

93. Kraus's most famous play was published between 1918 and 1922. *The Last Days of Mankind* is impossible to perform in full. Its 220 scenes call for a cast of more than 500. About a third of the text is assembled from speeches, editorials, news reports, military bulletins, etc. Since it deliberately overtaxes the means of the theater and since the characters speak primarily the language of public proclamations, the

certain abstractness of these products. And on the whole the theater of masks, as I mean it, is of a spiritualist character. Therefore it is perhaps (also) that only Jews will tend toward this theater.[94]

At the time[95] the opposition between comedy & tragedy was always worked out as an a priori division of the dramatic concept of space. And certain remarks could then be found puzzling, for instance that comedy deals with types and tragedy with individualities. In reality comedy & tragedy are no opposition as if the one were only that part of dramatic space that was excluded by the other. (Just as little as minor & major are such opposition.) Instead they are only two of many possible kinds of drama which only appeared to one particular—past—culture as the only ones. The right comparison is to modern musical keys.

A characteristic of theorists of the past cultural era was wanting to find the a priori where there wasn't one.

Or should I say a characteristic of the past cultural era was to create the 'a priori.'[96]

For it would have never created the concept if from the start it had seen the situation the way we see it. (A great—I mean, significant—error would then have been lost to the world.) But in reality one cannot argue like that, for this concept was founded in the whole culture.

That one person disdains the other, even if unconsciously (Paul Ernst[97]) means: it can be made clear to the one who disdains by presenting him with a particular situation which never occurred in

---

play calls for an adaptation by the puppet theater or a theater of masks. There is no evidence that Wittgenstein was familiar with the productions or writing of Edward Gordon Craig (1872–1966), who emphasized the relation between puppet and actor.

94. Compare *Culture and Value*, p. 1/3: "Tragedy consists in the tree not bending but breaking. Tragedy is something unjewish."

95. It is not clear what Wittgenstein's "at the time" refers to, though his characterization applies to most classical theories of drama from Aristotle through the nineteenth century.

96. See a remark dated February 27, 1937, in MS 157b: "The 'order of things,' the idea of the form(s) of representation, thus of the a priori is in itself a grammatical deception." [I.S.]

97. Paul Ernst (1866–1933) was a German novelist, an advocate of the strict, antipsychologistic form of the renaissance novella. According to Brian McGuinness, it is likely that during the 1916–1917 Olmütz discussions with Paul Engelmann, "Wittgenstein read or reflected on the *Nachwort* to the Grimms' fairy tales by Paul Ernst, which influenced him so powerfully with its account of how language misleads us—graphic modes of expression and metaphors being taken literally" (*Wittgenstein: A Life*, pp. 251f.). [I.S.]

reality (& probably never will occur) & he must admit that he would then act like this & that—& through this express his disdain.

If one wants to understand as Dostoevsky did the miracles of Christ such as the miracle at the wedding of Cana, one must consider them symbols.[98] The transformation of water into wine is astounding at best & we would gaze in amazement at the one who could do it, but no more. It therefore cannot be what is magnificent.—What is magnificent is also not that Jesus provides wine for the people at the wedding & also not that he gives it to them in such an unheard of manner. It must be the marvelous that gives this action content[99] & meaning. And by that I don't mean the extraordinary or the unprecedented but the spirit in which it is done and for which the transformation of water into wine is only a symbol (as it were) a gesture. A gesture which (of course) can only be made by the one who can do this extraordinary thing. The miracle must be understood as gesture, as expression if it is to speak to us.[100] I could also say: It is a miracle only when <u>he</u> does it who does it in a marvelous spirit. Without this spirit it is only an extraordinarily strange fact. I must, as it were, know the person already before I can say that it is a miracle. I must read the whole of it already in the right spirit in order to sense the miracle in it.

When I read in a fairy tale that the witch transforms a human being into a wild animal, it is also the spirit of this action, after all, that makes an impression upon me.

(One says of someone that, if he could, his looks would kill the opponent.)

When for a change the later ones of the great composers write in simple harmonic progressions, they are showing allegiance to their ancestral mother.

---

98. Wittgenstein here refers to part 3, book 7, chapter 4 of *The Brothers Karamazov*, where the story of Christ's transformation of water into wine (John 2:1–10) provides a mystical experience of never-ending joy to Alyosha. Compare Wittgenstein's remarks about the scientific and the religious attitude towards miracles in his "Lecture on Ethics" (*Philosophical Occasions*, pp. 43f.). [I.S.]

99. There is a nearly untranslatable play on words at work here. The German for "miracle" is *"Wunder,"* and therefore, *"das Wunderbare* (the wonderful)" means also "the miraculous."

100. Compare *Culture and Value*, p. 45/51: "A miracle is, as it were, a <u>gesture</u> which God makes . . ."

Especially in these moments (where the others are most moving) Mahler[101] seems especially unbearable to me & I always want to say then: but you have only heard this from the others, that isn't (really) yours.

Soiling everything with my vanity.

Through education (the acquisition of culture) the one simply comes into his own. He thereby gets to know as it were his paternal heritage. While the other acquires through this forms that are alien to his nature. And there it would have been better if he had remained uncultured no matter how awful & unpolished.

Fortunate is he who wants to be just not from cowardice but from a sense of justice, or from a regard for the other.—Most of the time my justness, when I am just, stems from cowardice.

By the way I don't condemn <u>that</u> justness in me which plays itself out on, say, a religious plane onto which I flee from the dirty basement of my pleasure & displeasure. This flight is right when it happens out of fear of the dirt.

That is, I am doing right when I proceed to a more spiritual plane on which I can be a human being[102]—while others can be human also on a less spiritual one.

I just don't have the right to live on that floor as they do & on their plane feel my inferiority rightfully.

I must live in a more rarified atmosphere[103] and belong there; & should resist the temptation of wanting to live in the thicker layer of air with the others, who are allowed to do so.

As in philosophy so in life we are led astray by seeming analogies (to what others do or are permitted to do). And here, too, there is only one remedy against this seduction: to listen to the soft voices which tell us that things here are not the same as there.

The ultimate ground (I mean the ultimate depth) of my vanity I won't uncover here anyway.

---

101. Wittgenstein wrote "Maler." For Wittgenstein's attitude toward the composer Gustav Mahler (1860–1911), see a remark from 1948 in *Culture and Value*. It begins as follows: "If it is true, as I believe, that Mahler's music is worthless, the question is what I think he should have done with his talent" (p. 67/76). But see also John King's recollection in *Recollections of Wittgenstein*, p. 71. [I.S.]

102. Compare Goethe's *Faust*, part I, scene 2, which celebrates the place where one can say: "Here I am human, here that's what I am allowed to be [*Hier bin ich Mensch, hier darf ich's sein*]."

103. Wittgenstein wrote "more raryfied atmosphere" in English.

When I am gripped by a tragedy (in the cinema, for example), I always tell myself: no, I won't do it like that! or: no, it shouldn't be like that. I want to console the hero & everyone. But that amounts to not understanding the occurrence as a tragedy. That's why I only understand the happy end (in the primitive sense). The downfall of the hero I don't understand—I mean, with the heart. So what I really always want is to hear a fairy tale. (Therefore my enjoyment of movies.) And there I am truly gripped & moved by thoughts. That is, as long as it is not frightfully bad it always provides me material for thoughts & feelings.

The photographs of my brother Rudi[104] have something of Oberländer, or more correctly something of the style of the good illustrators of the old 'Fliegende Blätter.'[105]

An English architect or musician (perhaps any artist at all), one can be almost certain that he is a humbug!

I can't judge the quality of a paint-brush, I know nothing of brushes & know not, when I see one, whether it is good, bad or mediocre; but I am convinced that English paint-brushes are outstandingly good. And equally convinced that the English understand nothing of painting.

The raw materials are always excellent here but the ability to form them is lacking. That is: The people have conscientiousness, knowledge & dexterity but not art, nor refined sensibility.

This is the state of my self-knowledge: When a certain number of veils is left upon me, I still see clearly, namely the veils. But if they are removed so that my gaze could penetrate closer to my self [*mein ich*], my image begins to blur for me.

I speak far too easily.—Through a question or an objection one can seduce me to produce a stream of words. While I talk I sometimes see that I am on an ugly track: that I say more than I mean, talk

---

104. Rudolf Wittgenstein (1881–1904) was the fourth child and third-oldest son of Karl and Leopoldine Wittgenstein. He was described as a nervous, anxious child, the one with the most literary sensibility. He was a student of chemistry in Berlin when he committed suicide at the age of 23, perhaps due to his homosexuality and problems of adapting to life in Berlin. [I.S.]

105. Adolf Oberländer was a caricaturist for the *Fliegende Blätter*, an illustrated humorous magazine that appeared from 1844 to 1944 in Munich. Famous contributors of text and drawings include Wilhelm Busch, Moritz von Schwind, Carl Spitzweg, Felix Dahn, Ferdinand Freiligrath, Emanuel Geibel, and Joseph Victor von Scheffel. Their humor typically targeted the forms of conduct of the German bourgeoisie. [I.S.]

to amuse the other, draw in irrelevancies in order to impressionate[106] and so forth. I then strive to correct the conversation, to steer it back onto a more decent course. But only turn it a little and not enough out of fear—lack of courage—& retain a bad taste.

This happens to me easily especially in England since the difficulties of communication (because of character,[107] not because of the language) are enormous from the start. So that one must perform one's exercises on a swaying raft rather than on solid ground. For one never knows whether the other has entirely understood one; & the other has never understood one <u>entirely</u>.[108]

> Five months have passed. During the summer, Marguerite had visited him for three weeks in Norway (Wittgenstein arranged accommodations to acquaint her with the simple life); they also saw each other almost daily near the end of the summer in Austria. See Monk's biography, p. 318f. and *Wittgenstein in Norway*, p. 43f.—The *Cambridge Reporter* announced that Wittgenstein would be in his rooms on October 10 to meet interested students; the term started on October 16.

12.10.31

Last night I awoke with dread from a dream & I suddenly saw that such dread means something after all, that I should think about what it means.

The dream had so to speak two parts (which however followed immediately upon one another). In the first someone had died, it was sad & I seemed to have conducted myself well & then as if upon returning home someone, namely a strong, old rural person (of the sort of our Rosalie[109]) (I am also thinking of the Cumaean Sybil[110]) gave me a word of praise & something like: "You <u>are</u> someone, after

---

106. The word "*impressionieren*" is self-exemplifying: It is used by that sort of people who are trying in vain to impress their listeners.

107. "Character" probably refers to "the English character" (shared by individual personalities) or possibly to the character of communication in England (social conventions and the like). See *Culture and Value* (July 9, 1948; p. 74/84): "It is important for our approach, that someone may feel concerning certain people, that he will never know what goes on inside them. (Englishwomen for Europeans)."

108. Compare the opening remark from 1914 in *Culture and Value*, p. 1/3.

109. Rosalie Hermann, apparently one of the Wittgensteins' housekeepers. In a letter on February 26, 1916, Hermine Wittgenstein writes to Ludwig of "good old Rosalie" being very sick, presumably on her deathbed. [I.S.]

110. The Cumaean Sibyl is a legendary Greek prophetess. According to Virgil (Book VI), Aeneas employed her services before his descent to the underworld to visit his dead father, Anchises.

all." Then this image disappeared & I was alone in the dark & said to myself—with irony "You <u>are</u> someone, after all" & voices shouted loudly around me (but I saw no one shouting) "the debt must yet be paid" or "the debt is yet unpaid" or something like that. I awoke as from a dreadful dream. (Hid my head—as since childhood I always do in this case—under the blanket & dared only after a few minutes to uncover it & to open my eyes.) As I said I became conscious that this dread has a deeper significance (even though in a way it came from the stomach, for that soon became clear to me), that is, that the capacity to feel dread is to mean something for me. Immediately after awaking, in dread, I thought: dream or no dream, this dread means something. I did something, felt something, after all, whatever my body was doing in the meantime.

That is, the human being is capable of such dread.—And this means something.

Also if a person experienced hell [only] in a dream & awoke afterwards, it would still exist.

Mine is a badly mannered (or ill-mannered) language.[111] That is, it lacks a good linguistic upbringing.—Probably like the language of most everyone.

Once read in Claudius[112] a quote from Spinoza in which he writes about himself but I couldn't quite come to terms with this reflection. And now it occurs to me that I distrusted it in one regard without being able to say really in what. But now I believe that my feeling is that Spinoza did not recognize himself. Thus, just what I have to say about myself.

don't blather![113]

---

111. There is a play on the word *"erzogen"* here: *"schlecht erzogen"* can also mean "badly educated," while *"unerzogen"* is also "unruly" or "ill-behaved."

112. The work of Matthias Claudius (1740–1815) was popularized by Karl Kraus. Claudius is best known for his poems in the style of plain folk songs. [I.S.] In part V of his collected writings from the *Wandsbeker Bote* (addendum to the second "Conversation about Freedom"), Claudius provides an extended quote from the fragment "The Emendation of the Intellect" in which Spinoza reflects on the conditions that led him to search for what is truly good (see vol. 1 of his *Collected Works*, pp. 7–11).

113. This appears to be the order of composition in this paragraph: First, Wittgenstein wrote, "He did not seem to recognize that he was a poor sinner. Of course I can write now that I am one. But I do not recognize it or else I would." The remark breaks off, he crosses most of it out with a wavy line, which expresses uncertainty or dissatisfaction. Alongside it, he writes: "don't blather!" He then continues by remarking: "The word recognize is misleading, after all, for it is a deed which requires courage."

He did not seem to recognize that he was a poor sinner. Of course I can write now that I am one. But I do not recognize it or else I would.[114]

The word recognize is misleading, after all, for it is a deed which requires courage.

One could say of an autobiography: one of the damned is writing this from hell.

In a sentence as much [as] has gone into it stands behind it.

Now I understand a little the feeling in my dream.

In that quote from Spinoza I am thinking of the word "wisdom" which in the final analysis appeared (& appears) a hollow thing to me behind which hides the actual person, how he really is. (I mean: hides from himself)

Uncover what you are.

I am for example a petty, lying rogue & yet can talk about the grandest things.

And while I am doing that, I seem to myself perfectly detached[115] from my pettiness. Yet I am not.

Self-recognition & humility is one. (These are cheap remarks.)

13.[10.31]

I don't want happening to me what happens to some wares. They are lying on the display table, the shoppers see them, the color or the sheen catches their eye & they handle the object for a moment & then let it drop back on the table as undesired.

My thoughts rarely come into the world unmutilated.

Either some part of them gets twisted at birth or broken off. Or the thought is a premature birth altogether & not yet viable in the language of words. Then a small fetus of a sentence is born that is still lacking the most important limbs.

The melodies of Beethoven's early works (already) have different racial features from for example the melodies of Mozart. One could draw the type of face which would correspond to the races. Namely, Beethoven's race is more stocky, with coarser limbs, a rounder or squarer face, Mozart's race with more delicate more slender & yet

---

114. The sentence breaks off here. The German still includes a "differently," which, in German, can precede the (missing) verb: "otherwise I would . . . differently."

115. Wittgenstein produces a self-exemplifying, detached expression by employing the foreign word *"detachiert"* for "detached."

rotund forms & that of Haydn[116] tall & slender of the type of certain Austrian aristocrats. Or am I here seduced by the image I have of these men's figures. I don't think so.

Strange to see how a material resists a form. How the material of the Nibelung-legends[117] resists dramatic form. It does not want to become a drama & won't become one & it surrenders only where the poet or composer decides to turn epic. Thus the only lasting & authentic passages in the "Ring" are the epic ones in which text or music narrate. And therefore the most impressive <u>words</u> of the "Ring" are the stage directions.

I am somewhat in love with my sort of movement of thought in philosophy. (And perhaps I should omit the word "somewhat.")

This does not mean, by the way, that I am in love with my style. That I am not.

Something is serious only to the extent that it is really serious.

Perhaps, just as some like to hear themselves talk, I like to hear myself write?

That something occurs to you is a gift from heaven, but it depends on what you make of it.

Of course such good teachings, too, are rightly <u>a</u> deed through which you act according to them. (In the previous sentence I was thinking of Kraus.)

Know thyself[118] & you will see that you are in every way again and again a poor sinner. But I don't want to be a poor sinner & seek in all manner to slip away (use anything as a door to slip away from this judgment).

My sincerity always gets stuck at a certain point!

Just as one seems to know quite well one's way about a hollow tooth when the dentist is probing it, so in the course of probing thought one learns to know & recognize every space, every crevice of a thought.

---

116. Wittgenstein misspelled the name of the Austrian composer Joseph Haydn (1732–1809) as "Hayden."

117. The German here is simply "*Nibelungenstoff*," that is, the Nibelung-subject-matter or material that goes back to the anonymous *Nibelungenlied* written around 1200 AD. The legends have been adapted to the stage (for example, by Friedrich Hebbel) and most notably by Richard Wagner in his cycle of operas.

118. To capture the Socratic dictum "*Erkenne dich selbst*," "*erkennen* (recognize)" is here translated as "know."

What I perform, so to speak (Kierkegaard),[119] on the stage in my soul doesn't render its condition more beautiful but (rather) more despicable. And yet again and again I take myself to be beautifying this condition through a beautiful scene on the stage. For I am sitting in the auditorium rather than viewing everything from the outside.[120] For I don't like standing on the sober, ordinary, unfriendly street but like sitting in the warm, pleasant auditorium.

Yes, only for a few moments I step out into the open & perhaps even then only with the feeling of being able always to slip back into the warmth at any time.

To be deprived of the affection of others would be altogether impossible for me because in this sense I have far too little (or no) self.

Perhaps I have a self only insofar as I <u>feel</u> <u>actually</u> reprobate.

And when I say that I feel reprobate, this is no expression (or just: hardly ever an expression?) of this feeling.

I have often racked my brain over my not being better than Kraus & kindred spirits & painfully reproached myself with this. Yet what an untold amount of vanity there is in this thought.

24.10.[31]

The secret of dimensioning an arm-chair or a house[121] is that it changes one's awareness of the object. Make this shorter & it looks like the continuation of that part, make it longer & it looks like a completely independent part. Make it sturdier & the other seems to rest upon it, make it weaker and it seems to hang on the other. etc.

It isn't really the gradual difference of length that matters but the qualitative difference of awareness.

---

119. "(Kierkegaard)" was inserted into the line. Wittgenstein may be referring to his *Repetition: An Essay in Experimental Psychology*. Kierkegaard draws on the theater as a metaphor and considers an audience that does not wish to remain in the auditorium but wants to go down to the street or wherever the scene is taking place.

120. The German *"auf dem Theater"* means "on stage." By writing *"derselben"* instead of *"desselben"* Wittgenstein appears to refer to the auditorium of the scene and not to the auditorium of the theater.

121. Compare Hermine Wittgenstein's memoir in *Recollections of Wittgenstein*: As the designer of his sister's house, "Ludwig designed every window and door, every window-lock and radiator, with as much care to attention to detail as if they were precision instruments, and on a most elegant scale. [. . .] Perhaps the most telling proof of Ludwig's relentlessness when it came to getting proportions exactly right is the fact that he had the ceiling of one of the rooms, which was almost big enough to be a hall, raised by three centimeters, just as it was almost time to start cleaning the completed house" (pp. 6–8).

If Brahms's instrumentation is accused of lacking a sense of color, one must say that colorlessness is already in Brahms's themes. The themes are already in black and white, just as Bruckner's are already colorful; even if Bruckner had for some reason written them down in one system only so that we knew nothing of a Brucknerian instrumentation.

One could say now: well then everything is okay for to the black and white themes belongs a black and white (colorless) instrumentation. But I believe that precisely in this lies the weakness of Brahms's instrumentation, namely in that it is frequently not decidedly black and white after all. Thus arises the impression that often makes us believe that we are missing colors, because the colors that are there don't have a pleasing effect. In reality, I think, we are missing colorlessness. And often this shows itself distinctly, for example in the last movement of the Violin Concerto[122] where there are very peculiar sound effects (once as if the sounds were peeling like dry leaves from the violins) & where yet one senses this as an isolated sound effect, while one senses Bruckner's sounds as the natural clothing of the bones of these themes. (It's quite different for Brahms's choral sound which takes root in the themes just as Bruckner's orchestral sound does in Bruckner's themes.) (The harp at the end of the first part of the German Requiem.[123])

Concerning the "secret of dimensioning": the real meaning of dimensioning shows itself in that one can give the object different names as its measured proportions change. (Just as, of course, with the expression of the face the proportions of which one has changed; "sad," "naughty," "wild," etc., etc.)

The joy I have in my thoughts (philosophical thoughts) is joy in my own strange life. Is that the joy of life?[124]

It is difficult to think nothing of oneself & to declare as delusional any proof that after all one may have a right to think something of oneself (proof by analogies), to declare this from the outset, even

---

122. Wittgenstein refers to Johannes Brahms's Concerto for Violin and Orchestra, D-major, opus 77. [I.S.]

123. Wittgenstein probably refers to the second of the seven movements of Brahms's *A German Requiem* for solo voices, choir, orchestra, and organ, opus 45. [I.S.]

124. Leaving out the parenthetical "(philosophical thoughts)," Wittgenstein copied this remark into MS 155; see *Culture and Value*, p. 22/20.

before one has seen through the mistake[125] (yes even if one should never catch on to the mistake).

31.10.[31]

The best prepared these days for the study of philosophy are students of physics. ~~(Not of mathematics.)~~[126] Due to the evident lack of clarity in their science their understanding is more loose than that of the mathematicians who are stuck in their self-assured tradition.

I could almost see myself as an amoral nucleus to which the moral concepts of other people stick easily.

So that, what I am saying is eo ipso never my own,[127] since this nucleus (I picture it as a white dead bundle) cannot talk. Instead, printed sheets stick to it. These then talk; of course, not in their original state but mixed up with other sheets & influenced by the position into which they are brought by the nucleus.—But even if this was to be my fate, I would not be relieved of responsibility & it would be sin or nonsense for example to <u>lament</u> this fate.

One could say: You despise the natural virtues because you don't have them!—But is it not much more marvelous—or just as marvelous—that a human being <u>without</u> these gifts can still be human!

"You make a virtue of necessity." Sure, but is it not marvelous that one <u>can</u> make a virtue of necessity.

One could put it like this: The marvelous is that what is dead cannot sin. And that what lives can sin but also renounce sin: I can be bad only to the extent that I can also be good.

I sometimes imagine human beings like balls: one out of genuine gold through & through, the other a layer of worthless material with gold underneath; the third a deceptive but false gilding and underneath—gold. Yet another where there is dirt under the gilding & one where in this dirt there is again a kernel of genuine gold. Etc. etc.

I <u>think</u> that I am perhaps the latter.

---

125. "Even before one has seen through the mistake" is an undecided alternative to "even before one has understood that it (the proof) is somewhere not correct." However, Wittgenstein's diary allows for different reconstructions here. Ilse Somavilla suggests that Wittgenstein's proposed alternative amounts to "even before one has seen through the mistake that it is somewhere not correct."

126. One of Wittgenstein's students at the time was the student of physics W. H. Watson. See the preface of his *On Understanding Physics*, p. ix.

127. Wittgenstein uses the Latin "*eo ipso* (due to the fact itself)."

But how difficult it is to judge such a person. One finds him out, [discovering] that the first layer is false & says: "so he is worthless" for no one believes that there can be falsely gilded genuine gold. Or one finds the trash under the false gilding & says: "Of course! That was to be expected." But that there should then still be genuine gold hidden in this trash, that is difficult to suppose.

When a cannon is painted to protect against air raids in such a way that from above it looks like trees or rocks, that its true contours become indiscernible & false ones have taken their place, how difficult it is to judge this thing. One could imagine someone who says: "so all these are false contours, therefore the thing has no real shape at all." And yet it has a real firm shape but it cannot at all be judged by ordinary means.

My sister Gretl once read a passage from an essay by Emerson[128] in which he describes his friend, a philosopher (I forgot the name);[129] from this description she thought she could gather that this man must have been similar to me. I thought to myself: What sport of nature![130]—What sport of nature where a beetle looks like a leaf but then it is a real beetle & not the leaf of an artificial flower.

In the correctly written sentence, a particle detaches from the heart or brain & arrives as a sentence on paper.

I believe that my sentences are mostly descriptions of visual images that occur to me.

Lichtenberg's wit is the flame that can burn on a pure candle only.[131]

"I can lie like that,—or also like that,—or best of all, by telling the truth quite sincerely." So I often say to myself.[132]

---

128. The essays by American philosopher Ralph Waldo Emerson (1803–1882) were widely read in Europe, for example, by Friedrich Nietzsche. On November 15, 1914, Wittgenstein noted in his "private" diary: "Reading Emerson's Essays now. Perhaps they will have a good influence on me" (*Private Notebooks: 1914–1916*, p. 96/97). [I.S.]

129. Wittgenstein's sister Gretl is probably referring to Emerson's 1862 funeral address for fellow-transcendentalist Henry David Thoreau (1817–1862). [I.S.]

130. Wittgenstein writes "*Naturspiel* (play, game, sport of nature)" and not the more familiar "*Naturschauspiel* (spectacle of nature)."

131. Best known for his posthumously published aphorisms, Georg Christoph Lichtenberg (1742–1799) was an experimental physicist and Enlightenment author of popular essays on scientific and philosophical issues. Two of Wittgenstein's friends pointed out similarities between Lichtenberg and Wittgenstein: Georg Henrik von Wright in his 1942 essay "Georg Christoph Lichtenberg als Philosoph"; and J. P. Stern in his book *Lichtenberg: A Doctrine of Scattered Occasions*. [I.S.]

132. In Dostoevsky's *Demons*, Stepan Trofimovich declares: "My friend, I have been lying all my life. Even when I was telling the truth" (part 3, chapter 7, section 2).

2.11.[31]
Dostoevsky once said that the devil nowadays takes the guise of fear of the ridiculous. And that must be true. For there is nothing I am more afraid of; nothing I want to avoid so <u>unconditionally</u> as ridiculousness.[133] And yet I know that this is a cowardice like any other, & that cowardice having been expelled everywhere has its last unconquerable citadel there. So that it is only seemingly defeated when it surrenders this place or that, since at last it can calmly retreat into this citadel & is safe there.

If I told people about me what I should be telling them, I would expose myself to the contempt & derision of nearly everyone who knows me.

"Rabble without a country"[134] (applied to the Jews) is on the same level as "crooked-nosed rabble," for to give oneself a country is just as little at a person's discretion as is giving oneself a straight nose.

The conscience burdened by guilt could easily confess; but the <u>vain person</u> cannot confess.[135]

I don't want to let myself become captive to a decision of mine unless the decision <u>holds</u> me captive.

Embrace someone for <u>him</u> & not for yourself.

7.[11.31]
Am quite worried now, through conscience & thoughts.

It is strange when two different worlds can live in two rooms one beneath the other. This happens when I live below the two students who make noise above me. These are really two worlds & no communication is possible.[136]

I now have the feeling as if I would have to join a monastery (inwardly) were I to lose Marguerite.

---

133. Wittgenstein is here referring to part 4, book 10, chapter 6 of Dostoevsky's *The Brothers Karamazov* where Kolya Krasotkin worries that people are laughing at him. Alyosha replies: "The devil has taken the form of that vanity and entered into the whole generation; it's simply the devil." See also Bouwsma, pp. 6f.

134. *"Vaterlandsloses Gesindel"* is a derogatory term that refers to all those who lack a fatherland, do not belong, or have no allegiance to the country in which they live.

135. The German language distinguishes between "confessing or admitting a crime" in a civil setting (*gestehen*) and "confessing a sin" in a religious setting (*beichten*). Wittgenstein uses the latter expression here.

136. According to Britton (pp. 709–15), Wittgenstein was then living at "H4 Great Court in Trinity" and then moved to rooms in Whewell's Court (where he lived in K10, on the top floor) after Christmas.

The thought of a bourgeois engagement for Marguerite makes me nauseous.[137] No in this case there is nothing I could do for her & would have to treat her as I would if she had gotten drunk, namely: not talk to her until she slept off her stupor.

It is true that one may be able to live also on the field of rubble from the houses in which one was once accustomed to live. But it is difficult. One had derived one's joy from the warmth & coziness of the rooms, after all, even if one didn't know it. But now, as one wanders aimlessly on the rubble, one knows it.

One knows that only the mind can provide warmth now & that one is not at all accustomed to being warmed by the mind.

(When one is chilled it hurts to wash & when one is sick in the mind it hurts to think.)

I cannot (that is, do not want to) give up enjoyment. I don't want to give up enjoying & <u>don't want</u> to be a hero. I therefore suffer the piercing & shameful pain of forlornness.

Despair has no end & suicide does not end it, unless one puts an end to it by pulling oneself together.

The person who despairs is like a stubborn child who wants to have the apple. But one usually doesn't know what it means to break stubbornness. It means to break a bone in the body (and make a joint where there wasn't one before).[138]

Old lumps of thought which a long time ago had already been pressing in the upper intestines come out later on some occasion. Then one notices a part of a sentence & sees: that's what I had always been meaning to say a few days ago.

The bourgeois odor of the Marguerite-Talla relationship I find so gruesome, unbearable that I could flee from it out of this world.

Every defilement I can tolerate except the one that is bourgeois. Isn't that strange?[139]

---

137. *"Bürgerlich"* means "bourgeois" as well as "civil." Also, the word Wittgenstein uses for "nausea" is old Viennese dialect: *"Übligkeit."* It would be another year (just before Christmas 1933) until Marguerite sent a letter to Margarete Stonborough announcing her intention to marry Talla Sjögren. The wedding took place shortly thereafter on New Year's Eve. [I.S.] When he wrote these remarks, Wittgenstein had not yet "lost" Marguerite.

138. Compare the very brief tale of "The Stubborn Child," #117 in Grimms' tales: After starving itself to death, it defiantly sticks its arm out of the grave which the parents then have to break.

139. One hour before Marguerite's wedding on New Year's Eve 1933, Wittgenstein called on Marguerite, imploring her: "You are taking a boat, the sea will be rough. Remain always attached to me and you will not drown." (See Monk, p. 339) [I.S.] See

I don't know whether my mind is sick in me or whether it is the body. I do the experiment & imagine some things different from how they are, & I feel that my condition would then return to normal right away. So it is the mind; & when I am sitting there listless & dull, my thoughts as if in a thick fog & feel a sort of mild headache, then this is supposed to come from perhaps—or probably—losing Marguerite's love!

When stuck in excrement, there is only one thing to do: March. It is better to drop dead from exertion than to die in a whimper.

Mind, don't abandon me! That is, may the weak flame of the spirit lamp that is my mind not expire!

There is something teasing about Kierkegaard's writings & that is intended, of course, even though I am not sure whether they are intended to have precisely <u>that</u> effect that they have upon me. There is also no doubt that one who teases me forces me to deal with his concern & if that concern is important, this is good.—And yet there is something in me that condemns this teasing. And is this only my resentment?[140] And I know quite well that with his mastery of it Kierkegaard reduces the aesthetic to absurdity & that of course he wants to do that. But it is as if there already were a drop of bitter[141] in his aestheticism, so that in & of itself it already doesn't taste like the work of a poet. He imitates the poet with as it were incredible mastery, but without being a poet & that he isn't one still becomes noticeable in the imitation. The idea that someone uses a trick to get me to do something is unpleasant. It is certain that it takes great courage (to use this trick) & that I would not—not remotely—have this courage; but it's a question whether if I had it, it would be right to use it. I <u>think</u> that aside from courage it would also take a lack of love of one's fellow human being.[142] One could say: What you call love for the fellow human being is self-interest. Well, then I don't know any love without self-interest, for I cannot intervene in the

---

also Misak (p. 349): Wittgenstein "confides in Lettice that he is in love with a Viennese lady, but he feels marriage to be sacred, and can't speak of it lightly."

140. The German use of the French word "*Ressentiment*" designates a sort of ill feeling or resentment that also involves envy.

141. The translation "drop of bitter" results from a perhaps unintended play on words by Wittgenstein: His spelling creates a hybrid of the words "*Wermut* (vermouth)" and "*Wehmut* (melancholy, wistfulness)" when he writes "*Wehrmut*." He goes on to write about the (bitter) taste from a single drop of vermouth.

142. The German "*Liebe zum Nächsten*" has a biblical ring: "*liebe deinen Nächsten wie dich selbst* (love thy neighbor as thyself)." "*Nächstenliebe*" is also translated as "charity."

eternal salvation of another. I can only say: I want to love him as I—who cares for my soul—wish that he would love me.

In a certain sense he cannot want what is eternally best for me; he can only be good to me in a worldly sense & show respect for all that seems to reveal in me a striving for what's highest. When I am thinking of my confession, I understand the expression ". . . & had not love etc."[143] For, even this confession would be of no use to me if it were made as it were like an artful ethical trick. But I don't want to say that I refrained from it because the mere trick was not enough for me: I am too cowardly for it.

(An artful ethical trick is something that I perform for others, or also only for me [myself], in order to show what I can do.)

I understand the mental state of my brother Kurt[144] perfectly. It was by only one degree even <u>sleepier</u> than mine.

The movement of thought in my philosophizing should be discernible also in the history of my mind, of its moral concepts & in the understanding of my situation.

Someone who must fight (against) (swarms of) mosquitos finds it an important matter to have chased some away. But that is quite unimportant to those who are not concerned with mosquitos. When I solve philosophical problems I have a feeling as though I had done something of utmost importance for all of humanity & don't think that these matters appear so immensely important to me (or shall I say: <u>are</u> so important to <u>me</u>) because they plague me.

15.[11.31]
A dream last night: I came into an office in order to—I think—collect payment for a bill. The room looked roughly like this:[145] a, b, c are desks d the door (not quite sure about c); a chair in front of both a & b an official was sitting in front of a and I stood to his left. Aside

---

143. Compare Luther's translation of Paul's first letter to the Corinthians 13:1: "*Wenn ich mit Menschen- und mit Engelzungen redete und hätte der Liebe nicht, so wäre ich ein tönend Erz oder eine klingende Schelle* [And if I talked in the tongues of humans and angels and had not love, I would be a sounding brass or a tinkling bell]." It is unclear whether at this time Wittgenstein actually made a confession as suggested by Drury who is not sure about the year 1931 (see Drury, p. 120). [I.S.] Again, Wittgenstein uses "confession" in the religious sense of "*Beichte*."

144. Kurt or Konrad Wittgenstein (1878–1918) was the second oldest of Wittgenstein's brothers. He is mentioned in letters (e.g., *Wittgenstein's Family Letters*, p. 31) and managed one of his father's companies. When during World War I his troop refused to follow his command and deserted, he took his own life. [I.S.]

145. The diary contains a sketch of the layout.

from me there was a very noisy bunch in the room, one of them sat in front of b & all of them spoke noisily & merrily to the official, & the man in front of b occupied in this a special position, such as translating jokingly for the official all that the others (who were standing near c) [were saying]. The official said he couldn't deal with them & turned to me. I gave him the bill & he asked who it was from. I would have liked to have said that it's written there anyhow & he should see for himself (for, he was holding the invoice in such a manner that he couldn't see the letterhead) but didn't dare say it and provided the name instead: Laval, or . . . de Laval. The official then inspected the bill by examining it in an electrical apparatus (I thought he took a picture of it with x-rays). It was in a sort of box which was wrapped in a black cloth. The scene had changed & the room was now like a small laboratory. On a big table stood the box with wires extending from it.[146] I was sitting on a chair almost like a criminal in the electric chair. The wires were coming toward me & then to the wall. I seemed to be coiled by them & ropes. I couldn't understand why I had to sit here like that. And said to the official: "the circuit doesn't pass through my body."[147] He: "of course not." I (annoyed): "But you have fettered me." He said thereupon that only my little finger was fettered, after all & "we do this to everybody." And now I saw that I wasn't fettered at all, for though the ropes & wires were draped in bows around me, they were not fastened anywhere else & only my little finger was tied by a string to a hook (at the table?).[148] I got up in order to try out my freedom & said a bit sheepishly to the official "I'm sorry"[149] I hadn't noticed that I was (completely) free. Then I woke up.

Immediately after awakening I interpreted the dream as a simile which I needed for my relation to Marguerite. Namely: it only looks as if I was bound to her by 1,000 ropes; in reality these ropes only

---

146. Again, the diary contains a sketch of the setup.

147. All the quoted dialogue was written in English.

148. The word "*Spagat*" means "string" only in Austrian. In German, the term is exclusively used to refer to "the splits" in gymnastics (and to be sure, the tied little finger in Wittgenstein's dream is doing the splits). Karl Menger noted that "*Spagat*" was one of a "few typically Austrian words, not understood in Germany" that were included by Wittgenstein in his 1926 spelling dictionary for elementary schools. See Menger, p. 84.

149. Wittgenstein first used indirect speech in German "that I am sorry (*es täre mir leid*)," crossed this out, and wrote, in English, "I'm sorry."

dangle around me but tie me to no one & only the small string is the bond between us.

What you have accomplished cannot be any more to others than you yourself are to them.

As much as it cost you, that much will they pay.

Christianity is really saying: let go of all intelligence.

When I say I would like to discard vanity, it is questionable whether my wanting this isn't yet again only a sort of vanity. I am vain & insofar as I am vain, my wishes for improvement are vain, too. I would then like to be like such & such person who was not vain & whom I like, & in my mind I already estimate the benefit which I would have from "discarding" vanity. As long as one is on stage, one is an actor after all, regardless of what one does.

In my mind I already hear posterity talking about me instead of hearing myself, the one who, because he knows me, is of course a far less appreciative audience.

And that is what I must do: listen not to another in my imagination but to myself. That is, not watch the other watching me—for that's how I do it—but watch myself. What a trick, & how infinitely great again and again the temptation to look at the other & away from myself.

Of religious offense one could also say: tu te fache, donc tu as tort.[150] For one thing is sure: You are wrong to be angry, your anger shall surely be overcome. And then there is only the question whether what the other one said is right in the end. When Paul says that the crucified Christ is an offense to the Jews[151] then this is certain & also that the offense is in the wrong. But the question is: What is the right solution of this offense?

God as a Historical Event in the world is so paradoxical, just as paradoxical as that a certain action in my life was sinful then & there. That is, that a moment of my history has eternal significance is no more or less paradoxical than that a moment or span of time in world history has eternal meaning. I may doubt Christ only insofar as I may also doubt my own birth.—For Christ has lived in the same time in which my sins occurred (only further back). And so one must say: If good & evil are historical at all then the divine order of the world & its temporal beginning & center is also conceivable.

---

150. "You are angry, therefore you are wrong." This Russian proverb is quoted by the defense attorney Fetyukovich in *The Brothers Karamazov*, part 4, book 12, chapter 14.

151. See I Corinthians 1:23.

But if I now think of my sins & it is only a hypothesis that I have performed these acts, why do I regret them as if any doubt about them was impossible? That I now remember them is my evidence & the basis of my remorse & of the reproach that I am too cowardly to confess them.

Saw photographs of the faces of Corsican brigands & thought: these faces are too hard & mine too soft for Christianity to be able to write on them. The faces of the brigands are terrible to look at, heartless, in a certain way cold & hardened; & yet they are probably no further removed from the right life than I, they are standing only on another side away from the righteous.[152]

Weakness is a horrible vice.

Between the previous remark and this one, Wittgenstein spent another Christmas vacation in Austria. Considering that his classes didn't begin until January 22, he arrived earlier than usual.

1932

11.1.32

Back in Cambridge after having experienced <u>much</u>: Marguerite who wants to marry me(!), quarrel in the family etc.[153]—But in the mind I am so old already that I must not do anything immature anymore & Marguerite has no idea how old I am. I appear to myself <u>as an old man</u>.

My philosophical work now seems to me like a diversion from the difficult, like a distraction, an enjoyment to which I do not devote

---

152. Wittgenstein copied this remark into MS 153b; see *Culture and Value*, pp. 13/15f.: "Am seeing photographs of Corsican brigands & think to myself: the faces are too hard & mine too soft for Christianity to be able to write on them. The faces of the brigands are terrible to look at & yet they are certainly no further removed from a good life & only situated on another side of it than I." [I.S.] See also Wittgenstein's discussion of faces recounted in Redpath's *Memoir*, p. 70.

153. The quarrel may have concerned a party for the sixtieth birthday of Hermine (Mima) Sjögren. She was a friend of Wittgenstein's sisters and the mother of his friend Arvid and of Marguerite's future husband Talla. His sister Margarete Stonborough had written a skit for the occasion, but Wittgenstein believed that this would gloss over the difficulties in their relation to Mima. He did not attend the party on November 29, 1931. See the correspondence in *Wittgenstein's Family Letters*, pp. 175–79.

myself with an entirely good conscience. As if I were going to the cinema instead of nursing a sick person.

One could imagine a person who from birth to death is always either sleeping or lives in a sort of half-sleep or daze. This is how my life compares to one that is really alive (I am thinking of Kierkegaard just now). Should such a one who lives half-asleep ever wake up for a minute, he will deem himself quite something else & he would not be disinclined to count himself among the geniuses.

Hardly one of my remarks that reproach me is written <u>entirely</u> without the feeling that at least it is nice that I see my faults.

28.1.32

How little regard I basically have for my own achievement shows itself for me in that I would accept or esteem only with great reservation a person of whom I had reason to believe he is in some other discipline what I am in philosophy.

Last night I dreamed the following curious dream: Someone (was it Lettice?) told me of some person that his name is Hobbson "with mixed b"; which meant that one pronounces it "Hobpson."—I woke up & remembered that Gilbert once told me, regarding the pronunciation of a word, "pronounced with mixed b"[154] which I understood as ". . . mixed beef"[155] & didn't know what he meant, that it sounded as if for the pronunciation of that word one needed to have in one's mouth a food called "mixed beef" & also remembered that I told this as a joke after understanding Gilbert. I remembered all that immediately upon waking up. Then it appeared less & less plausible to me & only in the morning when I was already dressed it seemed to me obvious nonsense. (By the way, if one looks into this dream it leads to thoughts about racial mixing and what is significant to me in connection with it.)

A soul that goes more naked than the others from nothingness through the world to hell[156] makes a greater impression on the world than the dressed bourgeois souls.

---

154. Wittgenstein wrote, in English, "it's pronounced with mixed b" and struck "it's."

155. "Mixed beef" is English in the original.

156. "From nothingness through the world to hell" is a variant on the "Prologue on the Theatre" of Goethe's *Faust*, which announces a journey "*vom Himmel durch die Welt zur Hölle* (from heaven through the world to hell)."

Marguerite can remain faithful to me only as her refuge. This she can & also should, when at some point she falls in love with another man. It would then become clear what I am entitled to with her. I can encourage her to remain faithful to me as her refuge; everything else would be taking advantage of her current predicament.[157]

My soul is more naked than that of most people & in that consists so to speak my genius.

Mutilate a human being all the way, cut off his arms & legs nose & ears & then see what remains of his self-respect & of his dignity & to what extent his concepts of such things still remain the same. We have no idea how these concepts depend on the ordinary, normal, condition of our body. What becomes of them when we are led by a leash with a ring through our tongues & tied-up? How much of a human being then remains in him? Into what sort of state does such a human being sink? We don't know that we are standing on a high and narrow rock & around us chasms in which everything looks completely different.[158]

The adoption of ancestral terms for coins "penny," "dime"[159] is characteristic for what Austria is today & also for the state of the European countries in general.

Tied up with that is the revival of folk dances & traditional costumes & a sort of move toward dopeyness.[160]

---

157. The final separation between Wittgenstein and Marguerite occurred only after her second marriage when, according to Marguerite, she received a letter from him that deeply offended her. In this letter (dated August 13, 1946), Wittgenstein expressed the wish that Marguerite might one day find work that would bring her together "with humans in a humane way" ("*mit Menschen in menschlicher Weise*") and "not as a lady." "Should you at some point have a decent job, or be looking for one, I would gladly see you again! Just not as a lady passing through. We would only depress each other." There is, however, one further letter from Wittgenstein to Marguerite, dated September 9, 1948, in which he thanks her for the "dear package" (according to Marguerite de Chambrier, it was probably a gift of chocolate). [I.S.]

158. Compare one of Wittgenstein's remarks on Frazer's *Golden Bough*: "But it may very well be the case that the completely shaved body induces in some sense to lose our self-respect. (Brothers Karamazov.) There is no doubt whatever that a mutilation which makes us appear unworthy or ridiculous in our own eyes can completely deprive us of our will to defend ourselves. How embarrassed we sometimes become—or at least many people (I)—by our own physical or aesthetic inferiority" (*Philosophical Occasions*, p. 155). [I.S.]

159. The examples in German are "*Groschen*" and "*Thaler*."

160. A literal translation of the German "*Vertrottelung*" would require a word like "dopeyfication."

My main movement of thought is a completely different one today from 15–20 years ago.

And this is similar to when a painter makes a transition from one school to another.

—Jewishness is highly problematic but not cozy. And beware if a writer stresses its sentimental side. I was thinking of Freud when he talks about Jewish humor.[161]

M. needs me as a corrective but not as her sole proprietor.

I sometimes feel as if my intelligence were a glass rod which carries a load & can break any moment.

My mind seems to be extraordinarily fragile then.

There is a space for thought in which, when falling asleep, one can sojourn further or not so far & when awakening there is a return from a greater or lesser distance.

Four and a half years have passed. Wittgenstein's fellowship at Trinity College had run out after Easter term, 1936. Starting in September 1913, Wittgenstein occasionally visited the Norwegian village of Skjolden. During the war, he had a cabin built for him that he occupied briefly for visits in 1921 and 1931. Wittgenstein moved there in August 1936 for his longest stay, with two interruptions, until December 1937. In the 1950s, it was torn down and the wood used to construct another house elsewhere. But in June 2019, it was reconstructed with the original wood on the original site in Skjolden.

1936

Skjolden 19.11.36

About 12 days ago I wrote to Hänsel a confession of my lie concerning my ancestry.[162] Since that time I have been thinking again & again how I can & should make a full confession to everyone I

---

161. Wittgenstein refers to chapter 3 of part A in Freud's *Jokes and their Relation to the Unconscious*.

162. On Ludwig Hänsel (1886–1959), see the appendix *infra*, containing some of his correspondence with Wittgenstein. Wittgenstein is here referring to the letter dated November 7, 1936; p. 115, *infra*.

Photo of Wittgenstein's house in Skjolden, Norway, taken by Dr. Ben Richards in 1950. *Credit:* Reproduction by permission of the Ludwig Wittgenstein Trust, Cambridge.

know.[163] I hope & fear! Today I feel a bit sick, chilled. I thought: "Does God want to put an end to me before I could do the difficult thing?" May it turn out well!

20.11.[36]

Weary & disinclined to work or really incapable. But that would not be a terrible ill. I could sit & rest, after all. But then my soul clouds over. How easily I forget the favors of heaven!

After having now made that one confession it is as if I couldn't support the whole edifice of lies anymore, as if it had to collapse entirely. If only it had entirely collapsed already! So that the sun could shine on the grass & the ruins.

The most difficult is the thought of a confession to Francis[164] because I fear for him & the horrible responsibility I then have to bear. *Only*[165] *love can bear this. May God help me.*

21.[11.36]

I received from Hänsel a beautiful & touching answer to my letter.[166] He writes that he admires me. What a snare! He refuses to show the letter to the other friends & relatives. I therefore wrote a longer & more comprehensive confession to Mining[167] today. Am tempted to think carelessly about it!

---

163. Wittgenstein had his written confession presented on Christmas as his family was coming together for dinner. Upon Margarete Stonborough's remark "Honorable people do not read another person's confession," no one—with one exception—touched it (personal communication by John Stonborough, but compare Hermine's letter; p. 119, *infra*). Wittgenstein also wrote to Engelmann and, in January 1937, sought out G. E. Moore, Fania Pascal, and Rush Rhees in England to confess his "sins." According to Pascal and Rhees, however, no one had ever been in doubt about Wittgenstein's background. Pascal writes in her contribution to *Recollections of Wittgenstein* that she never met anyone less capable of lying (pp. 37 and 177). [I.S.] Wittgenstein's correspondence with Hänsel shows that his Austrian family and friends were more likely to consider his confession a personal breakthrough of sorts.

164. Wittgenstein met Francis Skinner (1911–1941) in the fall of 1932. Skinner soon became his constant companion, perhaps the most intimate friend and intellectual partner he ever had. See Monk's biography concerning their relationship, especially pp. 331–34, 376–78.

165. Wittgenstein wrote this remark in code. This and later passages written in code are decoded and printed in italics.

166. See letter from Hänsel to Wittgenstein, dated November 15, 1936; pp. 115–17, *infra*.

167. "Mining" is the nickname for Wittgenstein's oldest sister Hermine (1874–1950) who remained unmarried and, after her father's death, took on the role of head of family. She cared in a motherly way for her younger siblings, especially for Ludwig, who referred to her as "by far the *deepest*" of his siblings (Rhees, p. ix). [I.S.]

Just as the screws are tightened, they become loose again, because what they are to squeeze together is giving way again.

I always take joy in my own good similes; were it not such vain joy.

You can't call Christ the savior without calling him God. For a human being cannot save you.

23.[11.36]

My work (my philosophical work) is also lacking in seriousness & love of truth.—Just as in my lectures I have also cheated often by pretending to already understand something while I was still hoping that it would become clear to me.[168]

24.[11.36]

Today I mailed the letter with my confession to Mining. Even though the confession is candid, I am still lacking the seriousness that is appropriate to the situation.

25.[11.36]

Today God let it occur to me—for I can't say it any other way—that I should confess my misdeeds to the people in the village here. And I said, I couldn't do it! I don't want to, even though I should. I don't dare confess even to Anna Rebni & Arne Draegni.[169] *Thus it was shown to me that I am a scoundrel. Not long before this occurred to me I had been telling myself that I was prepared to be crucified.*

I would like <u>so</u> much after all for everyone to have a good opinion of me! Even if it is a false one; & I know that it is false!—

It has been <u>granted</u> to me,—& I want praise for it! So instruct me—!

30.11.[36]

A storm is blowing and I cannot collect my thoughts.—

---

168. And see the end of Wittgenstein's letter to Hänsel, dated March 10, 1937, printed in *Public and Private Occasions*, p. 303.

169. Anna Rebni (1869–1970) and Arne Draegni (1871–1946) were two of Wittgenstein's friends and neighbors in Skjolden. Anna was a teacher in Oslo but returned to Skjolden in 1921 to run a farm and later the local youth hostel. Arne was a farmer on one of the various Bolstadt farms. Wittgenstein maintained a close correspondence with him after his 1936–1937 stay in Skjolden. What survives of this correspondence is published in *Wittgenstein and Norway*. [I.S.]

1.12.[36]

A sentence can appear absurd & the absurdity at its surface be engulfed by the depth which as it were lies behind it.

This can be applied to the thought concerning the resurrection of the dead & to other thoughts linked to it.—What gives it depth, however, is its use: the <u>life</u> led by the one who believes it.

For, this sentence can be, for example, the expression of the highest responsibility. Just imagine, after all, that you <u>were</u> placed before the judge! What would your life look like, how would it appear <u>to yourself</u> if you stood in front of him. Quite irrespective of how it would appear to <u>him</u> & whether he is understanding or not understanding, merciful or not merciful.

"White is also a sort of black."

Wittgenstein interrupted his extended stay in Skjolden by taking a trip to Vienna and London (and there to make some confessions). See Monk, pp. 367–72.

1937

27.1.37

On the return from Vienna & England, on the trip from Bergen to Skjolden. My conscience presents me as a miserable human being to myself; weak, that is unwilling to suffer, <u>cowardly</u>: in fear of making an unfavorable impression on others, for example on the doorman at the hotel, the servant, etc. Unchaste. Most heavily, though, I feel the charge of cowardice. But behind it stands indifference (& arrogance). But the <u>shame</u> I feel now is also no good insofar as I feel my outward defeat more strongly than the defeat of truth. My pride & my vanity are hurt.

With the Bible I have nothing but a book in front of me. But why do I say "nothing but a book"? I have a book in front of me, a <u>document</u> which, if it remains alone, cannot have greater value than any other document.

(This is what Lessing meant.[170]) In and of itself this document cannot "attach" me to any belief in the doctrines which it contains,—just as little

---

170. Wittgenstein is probably referring to Gotthold Ephraim Lessing (1729–1781), who wrote *Education of the Human Race.* See the note to letter 244 in the Hänsel-Wittgenstein correspondence, printed in *Public and Private Occasions*, p. 303.

as any other document which could have fallen into my hands. If I am to believe these doctrines I should do so not because this & not something else was reported to me. Instead they must be evident to me: & with that I don't just mean doctrines of ethics but historical doctrines. Not the letter, only conscience can command me—to believe in resurrection, judgement etc. To believe not as in something probable but in a different sense. And I can be reproached for my unbelief only insofar as either my conscience commands the belief—if there is such a thing—or in that it accuses me of depravities, which in some manner, that I am not aware of, however, don't let me attain belief. This means, so it seems to me, that I should say: You cannot know anything about such a belief now, it must be a state of mind of which you know nothing at all and which is of no concern to you as long as your conscience does not reveal it to you; whereas you must now follow your conscience in what it tells you. A dispute about religious belief cannot exist for you since you don't know what the dispute is about (aren't acquainted with it). The sermon can be the precondition of belief, but in virtue of what happens in it, it cannot aim to impel belief. (If these words could attach one to belief, other words could also attach one to belief.) Believing begins with belief. One must begin with belief; from words no belief follows. Enough.

- - - But aren't there various ways of being interested in ink & paper? Am I not interested in ink & paper when I read a letter attentively? For at any rate while doing that I am looking attentively at ink strokes.—"But here these are only means to an end!"—But surely a very <u>important</u> means to an end!—Yes of course we can imagine other investigations of ink & paper which would be of no interest to us, which would appear to us completely inessential to our end.[171] But therefore what interests us will be shown by our sort of investigation. Our subject is, so it seems, sublime & therefore, one would think, it should not deal with trivial & in a certain sense shaky objects but with the indestructible.

[I can observe on this journey a phenomenon that is uncommonly characteristic of me: Unless their appearance or demeanor makes a special impression on me, I judge people inferior to me: that is I would be inclined to use the word "<u>ordinary</u>" about them, 'a man from the street' & the like. Perhaps I wouldn't <u>say</u> this but my first glance at them says it. There is already a judgement in this glance. A completely unfounded & unjustified judgement. And it would

---

171. Cf. Wittgenstein's story about the value of a Rembrandt painting being assessed in terms of the value of the canvas and oil from which it is made (related in Hermine Wittgenstein, *"Ludwig sagt . . . ,"* p. 69).

also be unjustified of course if upon closer acquaintance that person really proved to be very ordinary, that is superficial. I am of course in many ways extraordinary & therefore many people are ordinary compared to me; but in what does my extraordinariness consist?]

If our considerations deal with word & sentence then they should do so in a more ideal sense than the one according to which a word can be smudged, hard to read and the like.—Thus we are led to want to consider the "representation"[172] of the word rather than the word. We aspire to something more pure, more <u>clear</u>, to something non-hypothetical. [My remark in volume XI refers to this.][173]

28.1.[37]

Still on the journey by boat. We were mooring at the landing dock & I watched the steel cable by which the boat was secured, and the thought came to me: walk on the cable; of course you will fall into the water after a few steps—but the water wasn't deep & I would not have drowned but only gotten wet; & most of all I would have been laughed at of course or considered a little crazy. I immediately shrank back from the thought of doing this & had to tell myself right away that I am not a free man but a slave. Of course it would have been 'unreasonable' to follow the impulse; but what does that say?! I understood what it means that belief is bliss for a human being, that is, it frees him from the fear of others by placing him <u>immediately</u> under God. He becomes so to speak an imperial subject.[174] It is a weakness not to be a hero, but it is by far a weaker[175] weakness to <u>play</u> the hero, thus not even to have the strength to clearly & without ambiguity acknowledge the deficit on the balance sheet. And that means: to become modest: not in a few words which one says once but in life.

To have an ideal is alright. But how difficult not to want to playact one's ideal. Instead to see it at that distance from oneself at which it is! Yes, is this even possible—or would one either have to become

---

172. In its philosophical meaning, the German word "*Vorstellung*" refers to mental representations; colloquially, it can also be translated as "idea."

173. Wittgenstein here refers to a manuscript volume now known as MS 115. While no corresponding remark could be found in it, similar remarks occur in *Philosophical Investigations* §§105–9. [I.S.]

174. Wittgenstein uses an arcane political term here. In the Middle Ages, municipalities were "*reichsunmittelbar*" if they answered directly to the emperor and not to an intermediary prince.

175. "Weaker" is an undecided alternative to "greater."

good or go mad over it? Wouldn't this tension, if it were fully grasped either open the person to everything or destroy him.

Is it a way out here to cast oneself into the arms of grace?[176]

Last night the following dream: I stood with Paul[177] & Mining, it was as if on the front platform of a streetcar but it wasn't clear that it was that. Paul told Mining how enthusiastic my brother-in-law Jerome[178] was about my unbelievable musical gift; the day before I had so wonderfully sung along in a work of Mendelssohn, it was called "the Bacchantae" (or something like this);[179] it was as if we had performed from this work among ourselves at home & I had sung along with extraordinary expressiveness & also with especially expressive gestures. Paul & Mining seemed to completely agree with Jerome's praise. Jerome was to have said again and again: "What talent!" (or something similar; I don't remember this for sure). I held a withered plant in my hand with blackish seeds in the little pods that had already opened & thought: if they were to tell me what a pity it is about my unused musical talent, I will show them the plant & say that nature isn't stingy with its seed either & that one shouldn't be afraid & just throw out a seed. All of this was carried on in a self-satisfied manner.—I woke up & was angry or ashamed because of my vanity.—This was not the sort of dream that I have been having very often during the last 2 months (roughly): namely where I act despicably in the dream, lie, for example, & wake up with the feeling: Thank God that this was a dream; & take this dream also as a sort of warning. *May I not become completely base and also not mad! May God have mercy on me.*

30.1.[37]

Feel physically sick; I am extraordinarily weak & have a certain feeling of dizziness. If only I could relate myself correctly to my physical condition! Still today I am like the small boy at the dentist's where I would also always

---

176. Recall the remark from October 22, 1930; p. 36, *supra*.

177. Wittgenstein's fourth-oldest brother, Paul (1887–1961), was a gifted pianist. After losing his right arm in World War I, he continued performing and commissioned concertos and chamber music for the left hand from Maurice Ravel and Sergei Prokofiev, Richard Strauss, Franz Schmidt, Josef Labor, Erich Wolfgang Korngold, and others. [I.S.]

178. Jerome Stonborough (1873–1938) was Margarete's husband. [I.S.]

179. *Culture and Value* includes numerous remarks on Felix Mendelssohn-Bartholdy (1809–1847). There is no work by Mendelssohn entitled "The Bacchantae." [I.S.]

mix up the real pain with the fear of pain & didn't really know where one ended & the other began.

Our object is sublime, after all—how then can it deal with spoken or written signs?

Now we speak of the <u>use of signs</u> as signs (& of course the use of signs is not an object; the object is what is real & interesting as opposed to the sign as its mere representative).

But what is there that is deep in the use of signs? What I am reminded of first here is that a magical role has often been attributed to names,[180] & second that the problems which arise through the misconception of the form of our language always have the character of the profound.[181]

Remind yourself![182]

31.1.[37]

Consider how the noun "time" can conjure a medium; how it can lead us astray so that we chase (back & forth) after a phantom.

Adam names the animals—

God let me be pious but <u>not</u> eccentric![183]

I feel as if my intellect was in a very unstable equilibrium; so as if a comparatively slight push would make it flip. It is as when one

---

180. See Fania Pascal's memory from 1935 (pp. 19–20): "I remember him picking up the volume of Grimms' tales and reading out with awe in his voice:

Ach, wie gut dass niemand weiss   [Oh, how good it is that nobody knows]
Dass ich Rumpelstilzchen heiss.   [That I am called Rumpelstiltskin.]

'Profound, profound,' he said. I liked 'Rumpelstilzchen,' understood that the strength of the dwarf lay in his name being unknown to humans, but was unable to share Wittgenstein's vision. To watch him in a state of hushed, silent awe, as though looking far beyond what oneself could see, was an experience next only to hearing him talk."

181. Recall the second paragraph of Wittgenstein's preface to the *Tractatus* and also 4.003. Writing for himself in 1931, in anticipation of a future book, Wittgenstein noted (*Wiener Ausgabe*, vol. 3, p. 266; June 20, 1931, in MS 110, p. 184): "If my book is ever published, tribute must be paid in the preface to Paul Ernst's preface to Grimm's Tales, which I already should have mentioned in the Log. Phil. Abhandlung as the source of the expression 'misunderstanding of the logic of language.'" Wittgenstein's friend Rush Rhees recalled that "Wittgenstein said repeatedly that he ought to have acknowledged this when the *Tractatus* was first printed" ("Introductory Note," p. 18). Wittgenstein's ongoing interest in Ernst is indicated by reference to him in the later *Big Typescript*: "The Mythology in the Forms of our Language ((Paul Ernst.))" (*Philosophical Occasions*, p. 196/197).

182. A page appears to have been torn out here. There is no indication of missing text, however, nor a break in Wittgenstein's page numbering. [I.S.]

183. *überspannt* (high strung)!

sometimes feels close to crying, feels the approaching crying fit. One should then try to breathe quite calmly, regularly & deeply until the fit is eased. And if God wills I will succeed.

2.2.[37]

Remind yourself at the right time when doing philosophy with what satisfaction children (& also plain folk) hear that <u>that</u> is the greatest bridge, the highest tower, the greatest speed . . . etc. (Children ask: "what is the greatest number?") It is impossible for such a drive not to produce various philosophical prejudices & therefore philosophical entanglements.

3.2.[37]

You shouldn't carry away the comforts of life like a thief. (Or like the dog who has stolen a bone & runs away with it.)
But what all this means for life!!

4.2.[37]

I may well reject the Christian solution of the problem of life (salvation, resurrection, judgement, heaven, hell) but this does not solve the problem of my life, for I am not good & not happy. I am not saved. And thus how can I know what I would envision as the only acceptable image of a world order if I lived differently, lived completely differently. I can't judge that. After all, another life shifts completely different images into the foreground, <u>necessitates</u> completely different images. Just like trouble teaches prayer. That does not mean that through the other life one will necessarily change one's <u>opinions</u>. But if one lives differently, one speaks differently. With a new life one learns new language games.[184]

   Think more of death, for example—& it would be strange if through that you wouldn't get to know new conceptions, new tracts of language.

5.2.[37]

Can't work for some reason. My thoughts don't budge & I am <u>at a loss</u>, don't know what to do in this situation. *I seem to waste my time here in a useless fashion.*

---

184. Cf. *Remarks of the Foundations of Mathematics* (revised edition), p. 132, Part II §23 (1938): "The sickness of a time is cured by an alteration in the mode of life of human beings, and it was possible for the sickness of philosophical problems to get cured only through a changed mode of thought and of life, not through a medicine invented by an individual."

6.2.[37]

An artist is "difficult to understand" in a good sense when the understanding reveals secrets to us, not a trick which we hadn't understood.

7.2.[37]

My writing is lacking piety & devotion again. So I am concerned that what I produce now might appear worse to Bachtin than what I have given him.[185] *How can anything good come from such stupidity.—*

8.2.[37]

The ideal name is an ideal, that is, a picture, a <u>form of representation</u> to which we are inclined. We want to represent the destruction & change as separation & regrouping of elements. One could call this idea in a certain sense sublime; it becomes sublime in that we see the whole world through it. But now nothing is more important than making clear to ourselves which phenomena, which simple, home-spun cases are the original picture of this idea. That is: When you are tempted to make general metaphysical statements, ask yourself (always): What cases am I actually thinking of?—What sort of case, which conception do I have in mind here? Now something in us resists this question for we seem to jeopardize the ideal through it: whereas we are doing it only in order to put it in the place where it belongs. For it is supposed to be a picture with which we compare reality, through which we represent how things stand. Not a picture by which we falsify reality.

Therefore we will ask again and again about that image for which we want to vindicate such general significance: "Where does that image derive itself from?!"

---

185. The brother of the literary scholar Mikhail Bakhtin, Nicholas Bachtin (1896–1950) came to Cambridge in the fall of 1932 to do a PhD. Bachtin was a classicist and linguist with wide-ranging interests who became a close friend of Wittgenstein's. Bachtin remained in Cambridge until 1935, and then held academic posts at Southampton and later Birmingham. Wittgenstein was a frequent visitor to Bachtin and his wife in Birmingham. Fania Pascal refers to Bachtin as "an intimate friend of Wittgenstein's." She quotes Bachtin's wife as saying "Wittgenstein loved Bachtin" and tells of "the interminable discussions that went on between the two men" (p. 14). A letter from Bachtin to Wittgenstein (*Wittgenstein in Cambridge*, p. 258; November 22, 1936) indicates that Bachtin was drafting a translation of Wittgenstein's work for him.

The "sublime conception" forces me to move away from the concrete case since what I say doesn't fit it. I now move into an ethereal region, talk of the <u>real</u> sign, of rules that must exist (even though I can't say where & how)—& find myself "on thin ice."[186]

9.2.[37]

A dream: I am riding on a train & through the window see a landscape: a village & pretty much in the background I see something that looks like two big hot air balloons. I delight in the view. They now ascend but it turns out that it is only <u>one</u> balloon with a parachute-like construction above it. Both maroon. Where it rises from the ground the ground looks black, as from the fire. But now I am also flying in a balloon.

The gondola is like a compartment & I see through the window that the other balloon[187] is approaching us as if driven by the wind. It is dangerous, for our balloon can catch fire. Now the other balloon is very close. I assume that the crew, which I imagine to be above my compartment, tries to push the balloon away from us. But I think it may have touched us already. I am now lying on my back in the compartment; & think: any moment a horrible explosion can happen & everything is over.

I am often thinking about death now & about how I will prevail in the anguish of death, & the dream relates to that.

13.2.[37]

My conscience plagues me & won't let me work. I have been reading in the works of Kierkegaard & that unsettled me even more than I already was. I don't want to suffer; that is what unsettles me. I don't want to let go of any conveniences or of any pleasure. (I would not fast, for example, or even restrain myself in my eating.) But I also don't want to oppose anyone & involve myself in discord. At least not as long as the matter is not placed right before my eyes. But even then I fear that I might dodge it. In addition an ineradicable immodesty dwells in me. In all my pitifulness I still always want to

---

186. This phrase is also used in *Philosophical Investigations* §107 as a metaphor for the faults of the sublime conception. Wittgenstein discusses the sublime with reference to the ideal, the real sign, and the original picture also in MS 157a and b. There, too, he arrives around February 8 at a point of dissatisfaction. See MS 157a, pp. 115f., 122, 130f., MS 157b, February 27, 1937, and thereafter; also cf. *Philosophical Investigations* §94, §101, §108f.; and *Culture and Value* p. 26/30. [I.S.]

187. Wittgenstein refers to his balloon as *"Ballon"* and calls the other *"Montgolfiere."*

compare myself to the most significant persons. *It is as if I could find solace only in the recognition of my pitifulness.*

Let me hold on to this that I do not want to deceive myself. That is, a certain demand which I acknowledge as such I want to admit to myself again and again as a demand. This agrees entirely with my belief. With my belief as it is. From that it follows that I will either meet the demand or suffer from not meeting it, for I cannot prescribe it to myself & not suffer from not living up to it. But furthermore: The demand is high. That is, whatever may be true or false in regard to the New Testament, one thing cannot be doubted: that in order to live right I would have to live completely differently from what suits me. That life is far more serious than what it looks like at the surface. Life is frightfully serious.

The highest, however, that I am prepared to carry out is: "to be cheerful in my work." That is: not immodest, good-natured, not directly untrue, not impatient in misfortune. Not that I am meeting these demands! but I can strive for it. But what lies higher I cannot or do not want to strive for, I can only acknowledge it & *ask that the pressure of this acknowledgment does not become too horrible*, that is, that it will let me live, thus that it does not cloud my mind.

For that, as it were, a light must shimmer through the ceiling under which I work and above which I do not want to rise.

15.2.[37]

Like the insect around the light so I buzz around the New Testament.

Yesterday I had this thought: If I disregard entirely punishments in the hereafter: Do I find it right that a person suffers an entire life for the cause of justice, then dies perhaps a terrible death,—& now has no reward at all for this life? After all, I admire such a person & place him high above me & why don't I say, he was an ass that he used his life like that. Why is he not stupid? Or also: why is he not the "most miserable of human beings"? Isn't that what he should be, if now that is all: that he had a miserable life until the end? But consider now that I answer: "No he was not stupid since he is doing well now after his death." That is also not satisfying. He does not seem stupid to me, indeed, on the contrary, seems to be doing what's right. Further I seem to be able to say: he does what's right for he receives the just reward and yet I can't think of the reward as an award after his death. Of such a person I want to say "This human being must come home."

One imagines eternity (of reward or of punishment) normally as an endless duration. But one could equally well imagine it as an instant. For in an instant one can experience <u>all terror</u> & all bliss. If you want to imagine hell you don't need to think of unending torment. I would rather say: Do you know what unspeakable dread a human being is capable of? Think of that & you know what hell is even though this is not at all a matter of duration.[188]

And furthermore, those who know what dread they are capable of, know that this is nothing yet in comparison to something even far more terrible which as it were remains covered up as long as we can be still distracted by externalities. (Mephisto's last speech in Lenau's *Faust*.[189]) The <u>abyss of hopelessness</u> cannot show itself in life. We can look into it only down to a certain depth, for "where there is life, there is hope." In Peer Gynt it goes: "An hour of this consuming strife is too dear a price to pay for life."[190]—When one is in pain one says something like: "These pains have already lasted 3 hours now, when will they finally stop," but in hopelessness one does not think "it lasts so long already!" for in a certain sense time does not pass at all in it.

Now, can't one say to someone & I to myself: "You are doing right to be afraid of hopelessness! You must live in such a way that your life can't come to a head in hopelessness, in the feeling: Now it's too late." And it appears to me that it could come to a head in different ways.

But can you imagine that the life of the one who is <u>truly just</u> also comes to a head only like that? Mustn't he receive the "crown of life"? Don't I demand nothing but this for him? Don't I demand his glorification?! Yes! But how can I imagine his glorification? In

---

188. Wittgenstein included a version of this remark in MS 157a; see *Culture and Value*, p. 26/30: "In one day one can experience the horrors of hell; there is plenty of time for that."

189. These are among Mephistopheles's final words to the dying Faust in Nikolaus Lenau's (1802–1850) *Faust* of 1836: "Once the stream of blood has subsided, the rush of which covered the secret, you can look down to the bottom and then behold your nature and mine." *Culture and Value* contains various remarks on Lenau; see pp. 3/5, 33/39, and especially three remarks from 1946 on p. 54/61: "I often fear madness. Have I any reason to assume that this fear does not spring from, so to speak, an optical illusion: of seeing something as an abyss that is close by, when it isn't? The only <u>experience</u> I know of that speaks for its not being an illusion, is the case of Lenau. [. . .] What is important is what Faust says about his <u>loneliness</u> or <u>isolation</u>." [I.S.]

190. These verses come from the second act of Henrik Ibsen (1828–1906) in his dramatic poem *Peer Gynt* of 1876.

accord with my feelings I could say: not only must he see the light, but get immediately to the light, become of one nature with it now,—and the like. It therefore seems that I could use all those expressions which religion really uses here.

These images thus impose themselves upon me. And yet I am reluctant to use these images & expressions. Above all these are not similes, of course. For what can be said by way of a simile, that can also be said without a simile.[191] These images & expressions have a life rather only in a <u>high</u> sphere of life, they can be rightfully used only in this sphere. All <u>I</u> could really do is make a gesture which means something similar to "unsayable," & say nothing.—Or is this absolute aversion to using words here some sort of flight? A flight from a reality? I don't think so; but I don't know. *Let me not shy away from any conclusion, but absolutely also not be superstitious!! <u>I do not want to think uncleanly</u>!*[192]

16.2.37

God! let me come into a relation to you in which I "can be cheerful in my work"!

<u>Believe</u> that at any moment God <u>can</u> demand <u>everything</u> from you! Be truly aware of this! Then ask that he grant you the gift of life! For you can fall into madness at any time or become unhappy <u>through & through</u> if you don't do something that is demanded of you!

It is one thing to talk to God & another to talk of God to others.

Sustain my intellect pure & unblemished!

I would like to be deep;—& yet I shy away from the abyss in the human heart!!—

I am writhing under the torment of not being able to work, of feeling feeble, not being able to live undisturbed by temptations. And when I now consider what others—who really were somebodies—had to suffer, then what I live through is <u>nothing</u> in comparison. And yet I am writhing under a comparatively tiny pressure.

---

191. The German "*Gleichnis*" has been translated as "metaphor" and "simile." Compare the "Lecture on Ethics" in *Philosophical Occasions*, pp. 42f.: "Now all religious terms seem in this sense to be used as similes or allegorically. . . . And if I can describe a fact by means of a simile I must also be able to drop the simile and to describe the facts without it." For remarks on religion and whether speaking is essential to it, see also Wittgenstein's conversations in *Wittgenstein and the Vienna Circle*, p. 117. [I.S.]

192. Regarding "uncleanly," see also Wittgenstein's comments from May 6, 1930; p. 23, *supra*.

What I recognize is actually: how terribly unhappy a human being can become. The recognition of an abyss; & I want to say: God grant that this recognition does not become clearer.

And I really can't work now. My source has dried up & I don't know how to find it.

17.2.[37]

Again and again I find myself dwelling on base *thoughts, yes on the basest thoughts. Hypocrisy of the most ridiculous sort & where it concerns what's highest.*

Just as one treads with fear on thin ice across deep water, so I am working a little bit today, as far as it is granted to me.

The horrible instant in an unblessed death must be the thought: "Oh if only I had . . . Now it's too late." Oh if only I had lived right! And the blessed instant must be: "Now it is accomplished!"[193]—But how must one have lived in order to tell oneself this! I think there must be degrees here, too. *But I myself, where am I? How far from the good & how close to the lower end!*

E.[194]

18.2.[37]

Have great longing for Francis.[195] *Fear for him. Would that I do what is right.*

Few things are as difficult for me as modesty. Now I am noticing this again as I read in Kierkegaard. Nothing is as difficult for me as to feel inferior; even though it is only a matter of seeing reality as it is.

Would I be able to sacrifice my writing for God?

I would much rather hear "If you don't do that, you will gamble away your life," than: "If you don't do that, you will be punished." The former really means: If you don't do that, your life will be an illusion, it does not have truth & depth.

---

193. In Luther's translation, "*Es ist vollbracht*" were Christ's last words on the cross. Wittgenstein wrote "*Jetzt ist's vollbracht!*" See John 19:30: "It is finished!"

194. Wittgenstein wrote "V." Ilse Somavilla conjectures that this letter might be in code and thus represents "E."—perhaps short for an ironically fitting "The End." It might also represent a roman numeral, indicate an intended insertion or continuation, etc.

195. Wittgenstein is referring to Francis Skinner.

19.2.[37]

Last night toward morning it occurred to me that today I should give away the old sweater which I had long intended to give away. But then, as it were like an order, the thought also came to me that I should at the same time also give away the new one which I recently bought in Bergen—incidentally without real need (I like it a lot). On account of the "order" I was now simultaneously in a sort of shock & outrage as so often during the last 10 days. But it is not that I am so attached to that sweater (though this plays some part, too) but what makes me 'outraged' is that something like this, & therefore everything can be demanded from me, & specifically demanded,—not just recommended as good or worthwhile. The idea that I might be lost if I don't do it.—Now one could simply say: "So don't give it away! what then?"—But what if this goes on to make me unhappy? But what does the outrage mean after all? Isn't it a rage against facts?—You say: "It can be that what is most horrible and difficult is demanded of me." What does that mean? It means, after all: It can be that tomorrow I feel I must burn my manuscripts (for example); that is, that if I don't burn them my life will (through that) turn into fleeing. And that through this I am cut off from the good, from the source of life. And perhaps through all sorts of antics dull myself to the recognition that it is so. And when I die this self-deception would come to an end.

Now furthermore this is true that I cannot through reflections make something right that appears as antics in my heart. No reasons of this world could prove, for example, that my work is important & something that I may & should do, when my heart says—without any reason—that I have to stop it. One could say: "The dear Lord decides what antics are." But I don't want to use this expression now. Rather: I cannot & shall not convince myself through any reasons, that my work, for example, is something right. (The reasons people would tell me,—utility, etc.—are ridiculous.)—Now does this mean, or doesn't it, that my work & everything else I enjoy is a gift? That is, that I can't rest on it as something firm, even regardless of the fact that it could be taken from me through an accident, sickness etc. Or more accurately perhaps: Now, if I have been relying on it & it was something firm for me & it is now no longer firm for me, since I feel a dependency which I hadn't recognized before (I am not even saying that I am now recognizing a dependency which I hadn't recognized before), then I have to accept that as fact. That which was firm for me seems adrift now & capable of going under. When I say I have to accept that as fact, I really mean: I must confront myself with it. I shall not <u>gape</u> at it in shock but be happy in spite of it. And what does that signify for me?—One could say, after all: "Take some medicine (or search for some) so that the idea of this dependency goes away." And I could imagine, of course, that it will go away. Also for example through a change of surroundings. And if one told me that I was sick now, this is perhaps also <u>true</u>. But what does it say?—This means, after all: "<u>Flee from this condition!</u>" And assume it ceased right now and my heart ceases to look into the abyss, able to direct its attention to the world again,—but this doesn't answer the question what I am supposed to do if that does not happen to me (for it doesn't happen through my wishing it). So I could of course look for a remedy for this condition, but as long as I do that I <u>am</u> still in the condition (also don't <u>know</u> if & when it will cease) & therefore am supposed to do the right thing, my duty, as it is in my <u>present</u> condition. (Since I don't even know whether there will be a future one.) While I can thus hope that it will change I have to accommodate myself to it now. And how do I do that? What must I do so that it becomes bearable <u>as it is</u>? What attitude[196] do I assume towards it? That of outrage? That is the death of me! In rage I only beat up on myself. But that is obvious! for, whom am I supposed to be beating with this? Therefore I must surrender. Any fight in this is only a fight against myself; & the <u>harder</u> I beat, the <u>harder</u> I get beaten. But it is my <u>heart</u> that would have to submit, not simply my hand. Were I a believer, that is, would I <u>intrepidly</u> do what my inner voice asks me to do, <u>this</u> suffering would be over.

What helps in praying is not the kneeling, but one <u>kneels</u>.

Call it a sickness! What have you said by that? <u>Nothing.</u>

Don't <u>explain</u>!—<u>Describe</u>![197] *Submit your heart & don't be <u>angry</u> that you must suffer so![198] This is the advice I should be giving myself. When*

---

196. Wittgenstein introduced the word "*Attitude*" as an undecided alternative to "*Stellung* (position)." The German use of "*Attitüde*" borrows from the French and refers to a general posture and stance, not to a particular view or opinion.

197. See §126 (also, §109 and §124) in the *Philosophical Investigations*: "Philosophy simply puts everything before us, and neither explains or deduces anything.—Since everything lies open to view there is nothing to explain." [I.S.] Various critics, most notably Joachim Schulte and Mark Rowe, relate Wittgenstein's "Don't explain!—Describe!!" to Johann Wolfgang von Goethe's morphological method. See R. Raatzsch, ed., *Goethe and Wittgenstein*.

198. The phrase "submit your heart" may originate from Tolstoy's paraphrase of the First Letter of John 3:19–21 in the conclusion to *The Gospel in Brief*. [I.S.]

you are sick, accommodate yourself to the sickness; don't be angry that you are sick.

This, however, is true, that just as soon as I can barely breathe a sigh of relief, vanity stirs in me.

*Let me confess this: After a difficult day for me I kneeled during dinner today & prayed & suddenly said, kneeling & looking up above: "There is no one here." That made me feel at ease as if I had been enlightened in an important matter. But what it really means, I do not know yet. I feel relieved. But that does not mean, for example: I had previously been in er-*ror. For if it was an error, what protects me against falling back into it?! Thus there can be no talk of error here & the overcoming of this error.[199] And if one calls it sickness once again there can be no talk of an <u>overcoming</u> for any time the sickness can overcome me again. *For after all, I also didn't say this word just when I wanted to, but it came. And just as it came something else can come, too. — "Live in such a manner that you can die well!"*

20.2.[37]

You shall live so that you can hold your own in the face of madness when it comes. *And you shall not <u>flee</u> madness.*[200] It is good fortune when it isn't there, but <u>flee</u> it you shall <u>not</u>, or so I think I must tell myself. For madness is the most severe judge (the most severe court) of whether my life is right or wrong; it is horrible but nevertheless you shall not flee it. For you don't know anyway how you can elude it, & while you are fleeing from it, you behave disgracefully, after all.

I am reading in the N.T.[201] *& don't understand many & essential things but much <u>I do</u> understand, after all. I feel much better today than yesterday. Would that it stay.*

One could tell me: "You shouldn't get so involved with the N.T., it may yet drive you crazy."—But why "<u>shouldn't</u>" I,—unless I felt myself that I <u>should</u> not. When I believe that <u>through</u> stepping into a room I can see—or find—what's important, what's true, then I can

---

199. See also Wittgenstein's "Remarks on Frazer's *Golden Bough*" (*Philosophical Occasions*, p. 121): "But this is not the case with the religious practices of a people and *therefore* there is *no* question of an error."

200. Wittgenstein frequently wrote about madness and his fear of going mad. Compare these remarks from 1944 and 1946 (*Culture and Value*, pp. 44 and 54/50 and 62): "If in life we are surrounded by death, so too in the health of our intellect by madness."—"Madness doesn't *have* to be regarded as a sickness. Why not as a sudden—more or *less* sudden—change of character?" [I.S.]

201. Wittgenstein writes "N.T." for "New Testament."

feel, after all, I should step in, no matter what happens to me inside & I shall not avoid stepping in out of fear. *Perhaps it looks ghastly inside, and one wants to immediately run out again; but should I not try to remain steadfast? In such a case I want someone to pat me on the shoulder & say to me: "Fear not! for this is right."*

I thank God that I came to Norway into the loneliness!

How is it that the psalms I read today (the penitential psalms[202]) are <u>nourishment</u> for me & the N.T. up to now really not? Is it only <u>too</u> serious for me?

The one who is innocent must speak differently & must make different demands than the one who is guilty. It can't say in David:[203] "Be perfect"; it doesn't say that one should sacrifice one's life, & there is no promise of eternal bliss. And the acceptance of this teaching requires—so it seems to me—that one says: "This life with all sorts of pleasure & pain <u>is</u> nothing, after all! It can't be there for these! It must be something far more absolute, after all. It must strive toward the absolute. And the only absolute is, to battle through life toward death, like a fighting, a charging soldier. Everything else is wavering, cowardice, sloth, thus wretchedness." This is no <u>Christianity</u>, of course, since, for example, there is no mention of eternal life here & eternal punishment. But I would also understand if someone said: Happiness <u>understood as eternal</u> can be achieved only <u>like this</u> & cannot be achieved by dwelling here among all sorts of small happinesses. But there is still no mention yet of eternal damnation.

This striving for the absolute which makes all worldly happiness appear too petty, which turns our gaze upward & not <u>level</u>, toward the things, appears as something glorious, sublime to me; but I <u>myself</u> turn my gaze toward the worldly things; unless "God visits me" & that state comes over me in which this becomes impossible. I <u>believe</u>: I should do this & that, & not do this & that; & all of this I can do in such a <u>rather dim illumination from above</u>; this is not <u>that state</u>. Why should I burn my writings today?! No way![204]— But I <u>do</u> think of it when the darkness has descended upon me &

---

202. The psalms are a collection of songs, prayers for different occasions, poems of wisdom which owe their origin to various authors, occasions, and times in Israelite history. There are seven penitential psalms (five of them attributed to David) among the 150 that have been divided into five sections. Perhaps, Wittgenstein was referring to Luther's 1517 edition of "The Seven Penitential Psalms." [I.S.]

203. The majority of the psalms in the Book of Psalms are attributed to David.

204. Wittgenstein here uses a colloquial expression: "*Ich denke nicht dran* (No thought of it)!"

threatens to remain there. Then it is as if I had my hand on an object & the object was getting hot & I had the choice between letting go & burning up. In this situation one wants to use the words of the penitential psalms.

(The actual <u>Christian faith</u>—as opposed to <u>faith</u>—I don't understand at all yet.[205])

~~Let me by no means flee that "madness"!~~ *but to* <u>*seek*</u> *it out that would be recklessness.*

Consider someone in horrible pain, say when something particular is happening in his body, yelling "Away, away!", even though there is nothing that he wishes away,—could one say now: "<u>These words are wrongly applied</u>"?? One wouldn't say such a thing. Equally, if, for example, he makes a 'defensive' gesture or rather falls upon his knees & folds his hands, one couldn't reasonably declare these to be <u>wrong</u> gestures. <u>This is just what he does</u> in such a situation. There can be no talk of 'wrong' here. Which application would be right if a <u>necessary</u> one is wrong? On the other hand couldn't one say, it was a right application of the gesture & <u>thus</u> there was someone here before whom he has knelt. Unless both of these statements are to have identical sense, & then the "thus" is wrong, too.[206] Apply this to prayer. How could one say of him who <u>must</u> wring his hands & beseech, that he is mistaken or in an illusion.

21.2.[37]

To get rid of the torments of the mind, that is to get rid of religion.

Have you not been somehow tormented in your whole life (just not in this way) & would you rather return to <u>*those*</u> *torments now?!*

I am good-natured but an extraordinary coward & therefore bad. I want to help people where no great exertion but <u>*most of all*</u> *where no courage is required. If this gets me into the* <u>*slightest*</u> *danger, I shy away. And by danger I mean, for example, losing some of the high opinion people have of me.*

The only way I could ever charge the enemy line is when I am shot at from behind.

---

205. In either or both instances, "*Glauben*" can also be translated "belief." Perhaps Wittgenstein aims to contrast faith and belief here, for example: "The actual <u>Christian faith</u>—as opposed to <u>belief</u>—I don't understand at all yet."

206. The second "thus" is not literally a quote of the preceding occurrence: Wittgenstein uses the synonymous terms "*deshalb*" and "*daher*." In this passage, the word "*falsch*" was translated as "wrong" instead of "false" or "incorrect."

If I must suffer it is better, after all, by way of a battle of the good against the bad in me, rather than by way of a battle within the evil.

What I _believe_ now:[207] I believe that I should not fear people and their opinions when I want to do what I consider right.

I believe that I should not lie; that I should be good to people; that I should see myself as I really am; that I should sacrifice my comfort when something higher is at stake; that I should be cheerful in a good way when it is granted to me and when not, that I should then endure the gloom with patience & steadfastness; that the condition which demands everything from me is not taken care of by the words "sickness" or "madness," that is: that in this condition I am just as responsible as out of it, that it belongs to my life like any other and that it thus deserves full attention. I don't have a belief in a salvation through the death of Christ; or at least not yet. I also don't feel that I am on the way to such a belief, but I consider it possible that one day I will understand something here of which I understand nothing now, which means nothing to me now & that I will then have a belief that I don't have now. — I believe that I should not be superstitious, that is, that I should not perform magic on myself with words I may be reading, that is, that I should & must not talk myself into a sort of faith, a sort of unreason. I shall not sully reason. (But madness does _not sully_ reason. Even if it is not its guardian.)

I believe that human beings can let their lives be guided _by inspirations entirely in all their actions_ and I must now believe that this is the _highest_ life. I know that I could live like that if I _wanted to_, if I had the courage for it. But I don't have it and must hope that this won't make me unhappy unto death, _that is_, eternally.

May gloom, the feeling of misery, somehow cleanse while I am writing all this!

I read again and again in the letters of the apostle Paul & I don't _like_ reading in them. And I don't know whether the resistance & revulsion I feel stem at least in part from the _language_, namely from the German, Germanic, thus from the translation. But I don't _know_ it. It appears to me as if it were not _merely_ the teaching which repulses me through its gravity, greatness, through its seriousness, but (somehow) also the personality of the one who teaches it.[208] It seems to me as if, aside from all that, there was something _alien_ & _thereby_ repulsive to me in the teaching. When, for

---

207. In his wartime diaries *Notebooks 1914–1916*, Wittgenstein compiled a similar list of his current beliefs; see pp. 72f. (June 11, 1916).

208. Compare two remarks on Paul in *Culture and Value* (pp. 30/35 and 32/37; October and November 1937). [I.S.]

example, he says "Far from it!" I find something unpleasant in the mere manner of the raisonnement.[209] *But isn't it possible that this would shed itself entirely if I were gripped more by the spirit of the letter. But I consider it possible that this is* not *unimportant.*

I hope that the present sadness & agony will consume the vanity *in me. But won't it come back very soon when the agony ends? And shall it therefore* never *end?? May God prevent this.*

In my soul there is winter (now) like all around me. Everything is snowed in, nothing turns green & blossoms.

But I should therefore patiently await whether I am destined to see a spring.

22.2.[37]

Have courage & patience even toward death, then perhaps you will be granted life! If only the snow around me would begin to regain beauty & not just have sadness!

I dreamt this morning: I am standing at the piano (indistinctly seen) & look upon a text of a Schubert song.[210] I know that on the whole it is very stupid, except for one beautiful passage at the end which goes:

> *"Entering knowingly*
> *my foothills,*
> *To you it became in an instant*
> *clear,"*

Then I don't know what comes & it closes:

> *"When perhaps already in the pit I*
> *am rotting away"*

What this means: When in your (philosophical) thoughts you come to the place where I was, then (it is supposed to mean) feel respect for my thinking when perhaps already etc.

Thank God that I feel a bit quieter & better today. But whenever I feel better, I am very close to vanity.

---

209. Wittgenstein emphasizes his distance by employing the French word for "reasoning" here. Luther uses *"Das sei ferne* (Far from it)" twenty-four times in his translation of the Bible, thirteen times in the letters of Paul (for example, Romans 3:4, 6, and 31; 6:2 and 15; 7:7 and 13; and 11:1 and 11).

210. There is no known source of this imagined Schubert song.

Now I often tell myself in doubtful times: "There is no one here." and look around. Would that this not become something base in me!

I think I should tell myself: "Don't be servile in your religion!" Or try not to be! For that is in the direction of superstition.

A human being lives his ordinary life with the illumination of a light of which he is not aware until it is extinguished. Once it is extinguished, life is suddenly deprived of all value, meaning, or whatever one wants to say. One suddenly becomes aware that mere existence—as one would like to say—is in itself still completely empty, <u>bleak</u>. *It is as if the sheen was wiped away from all things,* ~~everything is dead. This sometimes happens after a sickness, for example but of course it is not therefore less real or important, that is, not taken care of by a shrug. One has then died alive. Or rather: this is the~~ <u>~~real death~~</u> ~~that one can fear, for the mere "end of life" one does not experience (as I have written quite correctly). But what I have written here isn't the~~ <u>~~full~~</u> ~~truth either.~~[211]

In my stupid thoughts I compare myself to the highest human beings!

Really, the horrible that I wanted to describe is that one "doesn't have a right to anything anymore." "There is no blessing with anything."[212] *That is, this seems to me as if someone on whose friendly regard everything depends said: "Do as you wish but you don't have my consent!" Why does it say: "The lord is wrathful."—He can* <u>ruin</u> *you. Then one can say that one is descending to hell. But this is not really an 'image,' for if I really had to descend into an abyss this wouldn't have to be frightful. An abyss is nothing terrible, after all & what is hell anyway: that one could compare something to it, that is, explain it through this image? One must rather call this condition "a presentiment of hell"—for in this condition one also wants to say: It can get more horrible still: for all hope is not yet* <u>completely</u> *extinguished.* Can one say that one must therefore live in such a way that when one can hope no longer, one has something to <u>remember</u>?

Live so that you can prevail in the face of that condition: for all your wit, all your intellect won't do you <u>any</u> *good then. You are lost* <u>with</u> *them as if you didn't have them at all. (You might as well try to use your good legs while falling through the air.) Your* <u>whole life</u> *(after all) is undermined, and therefore you, with all you have. You hang trembling, with all you have, above the abyss. It is horrible that such a thing can be. Perhaps I have these*

---

211. Wittgenstein is referring to *Tractatus Logico-Philosophicus*, 6.4311: "Death is not an event of life. Death is not experienced [*erlebt*]."

212. There is no biblical source for this quote, but Psalm 109:17 (attributed to David) asks that the godless person be deprived of everything he had a right to: "As he delighted not in blessing, so let it be far from him!"

thoughts because I now see so little light here; but there is so little light here now and I have them. Wouldn't it be funny to tell someone: Don't mind that, you are only dying now because you can't breathe for a few minutes. With all conceit, with all your pride in this & the other, you are lost then, these don't hold you, for they are undermined along with all you have. But you should not fear this condition even though it is frightful. You shouldn't forget it frivolously & yet not fear it. *It will then give your life seriousness & not dread. (I believe so.)*

23.2.[37]

One kneels & looks up & folds one's hands & speaks, & says one is speaking with God, one says God sees everything I do; one says God speaks to me in my heart: one speaks of the eyes, the hand, the mouth of God, but not of the other parts of the body: Learn from this the grammar of the word "God"! [I read somewhere, Luther had written that theology is the "grammar of the word of God," of the holy scripture.[213]]

Respect for madness—that is really all I am saying.

Again and again I keep sitting through the comedy, instead of walking out into the street.

A religious question is either a question of life or it is (empty) chatter. This language game—one could say—gets played only with questions of life. Much like the word "ouch" does not having any meaning—except as a scream of pain.

I want to say: If eternal bliss means nothing for my life, my way of life, then I don't have to rack my brain about it; if I am to rightfully think about it, then what I think must stand in a precise relation to my life, otherwise what I think is rubbish or my life is in danger.—An authority which is not effective, which I don't have to heed, is no authority. If I rightfully speak of an authority I must also be dependent upon it.

---

213. Compare *Philosophical Investigations* §373: "(Theology as grammar.)" and Alice Ambrose's notes in *Wittgenstein's Lectures*, p. 32: "Luther said that theology is the grammar of the word 'God.' I interpret this to mean that an investigation of the word would be a grammatical one." G. E. Moore's notes of the same lecture (May 1, 1933; *Wittgenstein: Lectures*, p. 320) read: "Luther said: 'Theology is grammar of word of God.' This might mean: An investigation of idea of God is a grammatical one." Yet Moore then circles the second "of" in the first sentence and put a question mark by it. An editors' footnote to the published edition of Moore's notes indicates that Wittgenstein may have gotten this attribution to Luther from Johann G. Hamann's letter to his brother of February 19, 1760, where Hamann quotes Johann Bengal's report that Luther said that "The science of Theology is nothing else but Grammar, exercised on the words of the Holy Spirit."

24.2.[37]

Only if I am no (base) egoist can I <u>hope</u> for a peaceful death.

The one who is pure has a hardness which is tough to bear. That is why one accepts the admonitions of a Dostoevsky more easily than those of a Kierkegaard. One of them is still squeezing while the other is already <u>cutting</u>.

If you are not willing to sacrifice your work for something still higher, there is no blessing with it. For it attains its height only when you place it at its true altitude[214] in relation to the ideal.

That is why vanity destroys the <u>value</u> of the work. <u>This</u> is how the work of Kraus, for example, has become a "tinkling bell."[215] (Kraus was an <u>architect of sentences</u>, <u>extraordinarily</u> talented at that.)

It appears I am gradually regaining energy to work again. For in the last 2–3 days I was able to think more & more about philosophy again, though still little, & write remarks. On the other hand I have in my breast a feeling as if perhaps I was nevertheless not permitted to work. That is, while working I feel only tolerably or only <u>half</u> happy & have a certain fear that it may yet be prohibited. That[216] is, that a feeling of gloom might come over me which will render continued work meaningless & force me to give up work. But would that this not happen!!—But all of this is connected to the feeling that I am not <u>loving</u> enough, that is, too <u>egoistic</u>. That I care too little what feels good to <u>others</u>. And how can I live calmly if all the while I can't hope to die peacefully. *God, make it better!!*

"There is no one here,"—but I can go mad all by myself, too.

It is strange that one says God created the world & not: God is creating, continually, the world. For why should it be a greater miracle that it began to be, rather than that it continued to be. One is led astray by the simile of the craftsperson. That someone <u>makes</u> a shoe is an accomplishment, but once made (<u>out of what is existing</u>) it endures on its own for a while. But if one thinks of God as creator, must the conservation of the universe not be a miracle <u>just as great</u> as its creation,—yes, aren't the two <u>one and the same</u>? Why should I postulate a singular act of creation & not a continuous act of conservation—which began at some point, which had a temporal beginning, or what amounts to the same, a continuous creating?

---

214. "Place it at its true altitude" is an undecided alternative to "put it in its right place"—"altitude [*Höhenlage*]" resonates with the metaphor of the work "attaining height [*Höhe erhalten*]."

215. See Wittgenstein's earlier allusion to this passage in Paul's first letter to the Corinthians 13:1.

216. Wittgenstein started writing "I believe the reason is this," then struck this beginning.

27.2.[37]

Was away for 2 days with Joh. Bolstad,[217] *looking for a maid for Miss Rebni; without success. (It was nice & pleasant.) Now I am somewhat unserious; but—thank God—not unhappy.*

Christianity says: Here (in this world)—so to speak—you should not be <u>sitting</u> but <u>going</u>. You must away from here, & should not suddenly be torn away, but be dead when your body dies.

The question is: *How do you go through this life? —(Or: <u>Let</u> this <u>be</u> your question!)—Since my work, for example, is only a sitting in the world, after all. But I am supposed to go & not just sit.*

28.2.37

It is quite possible that after quite a few coherent chapters in my work I can <u>& should</u> write only loose remarks. I am a human being, after all & dependent on how it goes! But it is difficult for me to really acknowledge that.

1.3.[37]

I always want to bargain down the truth that I know & when it is unpleasant & again and again have thoughts with which I want to deceive myself.

Will it be granted to me that I keep working? I work, think & write some daily now, most of it only <u>tolerably</u> good. But is that now the <u>draining away</u> of this work or will the brook continue to flow, & swell? Will the work so to speak lose its meaning? I do not want that; but it is possible!—For first one must live,—then one can also philosophize.[218]

I think of eating all the time. Since my thoughts have arrived as if in a dead end, they return again and again to eating as to that which kills time.

In a hideous state of mind: Without any thoughts, gaping vacantly, my work means nothing to me &, I am here in the wasteland without rhyme

---

217. Johannes Johannesson Bolstad's (1888–1961) father was also a Johannes Johannesson Bolstad. Wittgenstein had built his house on the father's property and, in 1921, he bequeathed it to another son, Arne Bolstad. First a sailor, the younger Johannes Bolstad emigrated to the United States in 1907 but returned in 1929 to take care of his share of the family farm. [I.S.] See also *Wittgenstein and Norway*.

218. Compare the Latin proverb *"primum vivere deinde philosophari."* [I.S.]

or reason.[219] *As if someone had played a joke on me, brought me here & left me sitting here.*[220]

2.3.[37]
Today I fared better in my work; thank God. *There seemed to be some meaning in the work again.*

3.3.[37]
Yet how much easier it is to work than to assign to work its proper place!
　Kneeling means that one is a slave. *(Religion might consist in this.)*

4.3.[37]
Lord, if only I knew that I am a slave!
　The sun comes close to my house now & I feel gladder! I am doing undeservedly well.

6.3.[37]
I frequently copy to the wrong place Philosophical Remarks which I made earlier: there they don't <u>work</u>! They must stand <u>there</u> where they perform their whole work!
　It is interesting how wrong Spengler, who usually has much judgement, is in his evaluation of Kierkegaard. Here is one who is <u>too great</u> for him & stands too close, he only sees "the giant's boots."[221]—
　I know I am base & yet I feel much better than a couple of days & weeks ago. I am almost afraid of this well-being since it is so <u>undeserved</u>. *And yet I am glad. Would that I not be* <u>too</u> *base!*

8.3.[37]
I now have a great longing to see the sun from my house & make daily estimates how many more days it will stay away. I think that it

---

219. Literally, Wittgenstein's idiomatic *"Sinn & Zweck"* means "meaning & purpose."
220. *"Sitzen lassen"* is idiomatic for "standing someone up" or "leaving stranded."
221. In *The Decline of the West*, Spengler refers to Kierkegaard only once as someone who plays with religious expressions (see vol. 2, p. 137). That scholars are dwarfs between the feet of intellectual giants is a favorite theme of Schopenhauer's *Parerga and Paralipomena*, vol. 1, pp. 157f., 181; vol. 2, §§ 4–6, 248–54, 379f., pp. 535f., 542); also *World as Will and Representation* (vol. II, chapter 15; pp. 146–47) for a slightly different comparison. A definitive formulation of Schopenhauer's metaphor is offered by Nietzsche in the first section of his *Philosophy in the Tragic Age of the Greeks* (p. 32).

can<u>not</u> be visible to me for 10 days & perhaps not for 2 weeks, even though I told myself that I will see it in 4 days already. But will I live for another 2 weeks?? I must tell myself again and again that it is also <u>glorious</u> enough when I see its strong shine which I am seeing already & that I can be <u>quite</u> content with that. *This too is undeserved & I should <u>just</u> be grateful!*

10.3.[37]

I am doing undeservedly well.

12.3.[37]

I am a person with little talent; may I nevertheless accomplish something decent. For that is possible! I think.—Would that I were incorruptible! The valuable would lie in that.

13.3.[37]

How difficult it is to know oneself, to honestly admit what one is!

It is a tremendous blessing to be allowed to think, no matter how clumsily, about the sentences in my work.

14.3.[37]

I think the sun will shine into my window today. Have been disappointed again.

15.3.[37]

To know oneself is horrible,[222] because one simultaneously recognizes the living demand, &, that one does not satisfy it. But there is no better means to get to know oneself than seeing the perfect one. Thus the perfect one must arouse in people a storm of outrage; unless they want to humiliate themselves through & through. I think the words "Blessed is he who does not get angry at me"[223] mean: Blessed is he who can stand the view of the perfect one. For you must fall into dust before him, & you don't like doing that. What do you want to call the perfect one? Is he a human being?—Yes, in a certain sense he is of course a human being. But in another sense he is yet something <u>completely different</u>. What do you want to call him? don't you have to call him "God"? For what would correspond to this idea, if not

---

222. As opposed to *"kennen"* a few lines before, Wittgenstein uses *"erkennen"* here. *"Erkennen"* is usually translated "recognize."

223. Wittgenstein quotes Luther's translation of Matthew 11:6.

that? But formerly you saw God perhaps in the creation, that is, in the world; & now you see him, in another sense, in a human being.

Now at one time you say: "God created the world" & at another: "This human being is—God." But you do not mean that this human being created the world, & yet there is a unity here.[224]

We have two different conceptions of God: or, we have two different conceptions & use the word God for both.

But now if you believe in providence: that is, if you believe that nothing that happens, happens any other way than through the will of God, then you must also believe that this greatest thing happened through the will of God, namely that a human being was born who is God. Mustn't this fact then be of 'decisive significance' for you? I mean: mustn't it then have implications for your life, commit you to something? I mean: mustn't you enter into an ethical relation with him? For you have duties, for example, due to the fact that you have a father & a mother & weren't, for example, put into the world without them. Don't you therefore have duties also through & toward this fact?

Do I feel such duties, however? My faith is too weak.

I mean, my belief in providence, my feeling: "everything happens through the will of God." And this is no opinion—also not a conviction, but an attitude toward the things & what is happening. *May I not become frivolous!*

16.3.[37]

If you have found a valuable remark, & were it only a semi-precious stone, you must now <u>set</u> it correctly.

Today I thought: "Am I not arranging my thoughts as my sister Gretl does the furniture in a room?" And at first I found this thought unpleasant.

Yesterday I thought of the expression: "a pure heart";[225] why don't I have one? That means, after all: why are my thoughts so impure! In my thoughts there is again and again vanity, swindle, resentment. May God steer my life so that it becomes different.

---

224. In his conversations *Wittgenstein and the Vienna Circle* (on December 17, 1930, p. 118), Waismann asked Wittgenstein: "Is the existence of the world connected with what is ethical?" Wittgenstein responded: "Men have felt that there is a connection and they have expressed it thus: God the Father created the world, the Son of God (or the Word that comes from God) is that which is ethical. That the Godhead is thought of as divided and, again, as one being indicates that there is a connection here." [I.S.]

225. Compare Matthew 5:8: "Blessed are the pure in heart, for they shall see God." [I.S.]

17.3.[37]

Because of the clouds it is impossible to see whether the sun is above the mountain already or not yet & I am almost sick from the longing to finally see it. (I want to quarrel with God.)

18.3.[37]

The sun should be above the mountain now but is invisible because of the weather. If you want to quarrel with God, that means that you have a false concept of God. You are superstitious. You have an incorrect concept when you get angry with fate. You should rearrange your concepts. Contentment with your fate ought to be the first command of wisdom.

Today I saw the sun from my window at the moment when it started rising from behind the western mountain. Thank God. <u>But to my shame I now believe that this word</u>[226] <u>was not sufficiently heartfelt</u>. For I was quite glad when I <u>really</u> saw the sun but my joy was not deep enough, too merry, not truly religious. *Oh, if only I were deeper!*

19.3.[37]

About 20 minutes after 12 the rim of the sun now shows itself. It moves along the edge of the mountain so that it is only partially visible, half of it or less, or more. Only for very few moments it was <u>almost</u> completely visible. And that shows that, after all, it first crossed the horizon only yesterday; if not for the first time today. At 1pm it had set already. And now it comes once more just before setting.

20.3.[37]

I believe: I understand that the state of mind of believing can make the human being blissful. For when people believe, <u>wholeheartedly</u> believe, that the perfect one has sacrificed himself for them, that he has therefore—from the beginning—reconciled them with God, so that from now on you shall simply live in a way that is worthy of this sacrifice,—then this must refine the whole person, elevate him to nobility, so to speak. I understand—I want to say—that this <u>is</u> a movement of the soul toward bliss.

---

226. Wittgenstein drew an arrow from "word" to "God," perhaps indicating that the whole expression "thank God" was less than heartfelt.

It is written—I believe—"Believe that you are now reconciled, & don't sin 'henceforth any more'!"[227]—But it is also clear that this belief is a blessing. And, I believe, the condition for it is that we do our utmost & see that it leads us nowhere, that, no matter how much we torment ourselves, we remain unreconciled. Then the reconciliation comes rightfully. But now, is that person lost who is not of this belief? I can't believe that; or rather can't believe it yet. For perhaps I will believe it. If one is speaking here of the 'secret' of that sacrifice: you would have to understand the grammar of the word "secret" here!

There is no one here: & yet I speak & thank & petition. But is this speaking & thanking & petitioning an error?!

I would rather say: "This is what's strange!"

In doubt what to do in the immediate future. An inner voice tells me that I should now get away from here, & to Dublin. But then again I hope that I won't have to do this now. I would like to say: Would that I am granted that I can work here some more time!—But I have, so to speak, arrived at the end of a section of my work.

God, what a blessing it is to be able to live without horrible problems! Would that it stays with me!

21.3.[37]

Am base & low & doing all too well. And yet I am glad that I am not doing worse! Dear letter from Max.[228]

22.3.[37]

Today the sun rises here at 12 noon & now appears completely.

This morning the trees were thickly loaded with snow, now all of it is melting.—Again & again I tend toward vanity, also regarding my entries here & their style. May God improve this.—*The first fly outside the window where the sun shines on it. At 1pm the sun sets again*

---

227. Compare John 5:14 and 8:11; but see also Romans 5 and 6 on reconciliation. [I.S.]

228. Max Salzer (1868–1941) was the husband of Wittgenstein's sister Helene. He was a ministry official at the highest rank. His letter is printed in *Wittgenstein's Family Letters* (pp. 212–13). Wittgenstein's reply to his letter (p. 213, dated March 23) reads, in part: "I've been meaning to tell you that a wee thing of a book written by me will be published in the near future, entitled *The Philosopher's Handbook*, dedicated to you and your wife. It will be printed on thin hygienic paper with non-bleeding printer ink, and every sheet can be ripped out individually."

& however shows itself once more. Before it sets the sun can be seen once more for about 10 minutes.

There is no one here: But there is a <u>glorious</u> sun here, & a <u>bad</u> person. —

23.3.[37]

I am like a beggar who sometimes reluctantly admits that he is no king.

Today the sun showed itself above the mountain from roughly 11:45 until 1:15, then a moment at 3:45 & before it sets it shines in again.

Help & illuminate! But if I believe something tomorrow that I don't believe today, I was not therefore in an error today. For this 'believing' is not <u>holding an opinion,</u> after all. But my belief tomorrow can be <u>lighter</u> (or darker) than my belief today. *Help & illuminate!* & would that no darkness descend upon me!

24.3.[37]

I am petitioning & *I already have it as I want to have it: namely half heaven, half hell!*

The sun sets at about 1:30 but then moves along the mountain ridge so that for quite some time one still perceives its outermost ridge. It is glorious! So it hasn't really set after all.—

I had this thought today: At the time when I had written down my confession I thought a few times also of my mom[229] & thought that I could in some sense retroactively redeem her through my confession;[230] for I thought she, too, was carrying such a confession in her heart & hadn't unburdened it in her life for she remained withdrawn. And my confession, so it seemed to me, was finally

---

229. Leopoldine (Poldy) Wittgenstein, née Kallmus (1850–1926) was a sophisticated woman whose primary love was music. She played the piano and organ exceedingly well and was considered a stern critic. Rudolf Koder maintained that she played her piano better even than her son Paul, the pianist (as reported by John Stonborough to Ilse Somavilla). Hermine Wittgenstein writes this about her mother in her *Familienerinnerungen* (p. 132): "And yet I saw or felt clearly that my mother did straightforwardly what she recognized to be right and good, that in doing so she never considered her own wishes, indeed, didn't appear to have any. [. . .] She never spared herself, was rather very hard on herself and hid all pain especially from her husband and her mother." [I.S.]

230. The German language distinguishes between two kinds of confession. In this sentence, Wittgenstein first uses *"Beichte* (religious confession, the confession of sins)." The second and the next two occurrences refer to a *"Geständnis* (civil confession, the confession of a crime)."

speaking in her name, too; & she could now somehow identify with it retroactively. (It would be as if I paid the debt that already burdened her & as if her spirit could tell me: "Thank God that you paid it off now.")—Now, I was thinking outside today about the meaning of the doctrine of the redemptive death & I thought: Might the re-

25.3.[37][231]

demption through the sacrifice consist in the fact that <u>he has done</u> what all of us want to, but can't do. But in believing one identifies with <u>him</u>, that is, one pays the debt now in the form of humble recognition; one shall therefore become quite <u>abject</u> because one can't become good.

The thought occurred to me that I should fast tomorrow (on Good Friday) & I thought: I will do that. But immediately afterwards it appeared to me like a commandment, as if I <u>had</u> to do it & I resisted that. I said: "I want to do it if it comes from my heart & not because I was <u>commanded</u> to." But this then is no obedience! There is no <u>mortification</u> in doing what comes from the heart (even if it is friendly or in some sense pious). You don't <u>die</u> in this, after all. Whereas you <u>die</u> precisely in obedience towards a command, from mere obedience. This is agony but can be, is supposed to be, a pious agony. That's at least how I understand it. But I myself!—I confess that I do not want to die off, even though I understand that it is the higher. *This is horrible; & may this horribleness become illuminated by the light shining in!*

Have been sleeping quite badly for a few nights & feel dead, can't work; my thoughts are dim & I am depressed but in a glowering way. (That is, I am afraid of certain religious thoughts.)

26.3.[37]

Don't criticize what serious people have written seriously, for you don't know what you are criticizing. Why should you form an opinion about everything. But that doesn't mean: agree with all that.

I am as illuminated as I am; I mean: my religion is as illuminated as it is. <u>I</u> haven't illuminated myself less yesterday & not more today. For had I been <u>able</u> to view it like that yesterday, I would have definitely viewed it like that.

One shouldn't be puzzled that one age doesn't believe in witches & a later one does believe in witches & that this & similar things go

---

231. Wittgenstein added the date by putting it into the top-margin of the page.

away & come back, etc.; but in order to no longer be puzzled you only need to look at what happens to yourself.—One day you can pray but on another perhaps not, & one day you <u>must</u> pray, & on another not.

Through mercy I am doing much better today than yesterday.

27.3.[37]

The sun comes up just after 11am now & is radiant today. I find it hard not to look into it again and again, that is, I want to look into it again and again even though I know that it is bad for my eyes.

30.3.[37]

Beware of cheap poignancy[232] when writing about philosophy! I am always in danger of that when <u>little</u> occurs to me. And so it is now. I have come to a curious standstill & don't quite know what to do.

Starting today the sun now shines in from 10:30 until 5:30 without interruption & the weather is glorious.

I had hoped my capacity to work would recover when I saw more of the sun, but it didn't turn out that way.

2.4.[37]

My brain makes only rather sluggish movements. Unfortunately.

4.4.[37]

I easily tire from my work now; or am I sluggish?—I sometimes consider whether I should now already leave from here. For example: first to Vienna for a month, then to England for a month— or longer—then to Russia.[233] And then return here again?—Or to Ireland?[234] What <u>now</u> appears most prudent to me is to leave here in about 3 weeks.—

---

232. The German word is "*Pathos*," which signifies grand emotional gestures.

233. In September 1935, Wittgenstein had traveled to Russia, planning to stay for a while doing simple labor on a collective farm. When he was only offered a position at a university, he left Russia at the beginning of October. Here we find him almost two years later talking about Russia again, and on June 21 of the same year, he would write to Paul Engelmann: "I am now in England for a short stay; perhaps I shall go to Russia. God knows what will become of me" (*Letters from Ludwig Wittgenstein*, p. 59). Compare Monk, pp. 248, 342f., 347–54. [I.S.]

234. Wittgenstein had gone to Dublin in August 1936 to visit his friend Maurice O'Connor Drury. At the time, he considered studying medicine and then to start a joint psychiatric practice with Drury. Later, he would frequently travel to Ireland (in the years 1947–1949). [I.S.]

5.4.[37]

Would that I see life as it is. That is, see it more as a whole, & not just a small, tiny section of it, I mean, for example: my work. It is then as if everything else was dimmed by a dark screen & only this piece visible. Because of that everything appears wrongly. I see, feel the value of things wrongly.

I don't know at all what I should do in the future. Shall I return here, to Skjolden? And do what here, when I am not able to work here? Should I live here also without work? And without regular work,—I can't do that. Or shall I <u>absolutely</u> attempt to work? If that, I must do that <u>now</u> too!

I am convinced I am looking at everything wrongly when I speculate like that.

Has my Norwegian stay <u>done</u> its job?[235] For it can't be right that it degenerates into a sort of half-comfortable, half-uncomfortable hermit's life. It must bear fruit!—There would be the possibility, after all, to stay here much longer <u>now</u>, to postpone my arrival in Vienna & England. And the question is: Could I resolve to stay here, say, for another <u>two</u> months? God, <u>I believe yes</u>! It's just that I worry about my friend[236] & don't want to disappoint my people in Vienna. <u>I believe</u> I can take it upon myself to stay here if I can be here <u>whole-</u>heartedly, if my task is <u>simply</u> to stay here, & to await <u>whether</u> I will be able to work well.

On the other hand it is true that something drives me away from here. I am feeling dull, want to get away & return fresh after a while.—One thing is for sure, I very quickly tire now in my work & this is not my fault. After a few hours of not very intense work I can't think anymore. It is as if I were tired now. Am I lacking the correct nourishment? That would be possible.

---

235. Compare this entry of August 19, 1937, in MS 118, p. 5f.: "I am feeling very strange; I don't know whether I have a right or good reason to live here now. I have no real need of loneliness, nor an overwhelming drive to work. One voice says: wait a little, then it will show itself.—Another voice is saying: Impossible that you will be able to endure here! But what shall I do? To Cambridge? I won't be able to write there. [. . .] One thing is clear: I am <u>here</u> now—no matter how and why I came here. So let me utilize my being-here as far as it goes. [. . .] That is, I can stay roughly 6 weeks, <u>no matter how</u> my work might go, but if after this time I have no <u>clear</u> reason for assuming that I work better here than elsewhere, then it is time to go. May God grant that I utilize my time of being-here well!" [I.S.]

236. Wittgenstein is probably referring to Francis Skinner.

6.4.[37]

An exegesis of the Christian teaching: Wake up completely! When you do that you recognize that you are no good & thus the joy you take in this world comes to an end. And it can't come back either if you <u>stay</u> awake. But now you need <u>salvation</u>,—otherwise you are lost. But you must stay alive (and this world is dead to you) so you need a new light from elsewhere. In this light there can be no cleverness, wisdom; for to this world you are dead. (Since this world is the paradise in which, because of your sinfulness, you can't go about anything, however.) You must acknowledge yourself as dead & receive <u>another</u> life (for without that it is impossible to acknowledge yourself as dead without despair). This life must uphold you as if in suspension above this earth; that is, when you are walking on the earth, you nevertheless no longer <u>rest</u> on the earth, but <u>hang</u> in the sky;[237] you are held from <u>above</u>, not supported from below.—But this life is love, human love, of the perfect one.[238] And <u>this love</u> is faith.

"Everything else works itself out."[239]

God be praised that I am clearer today & feeling better.

Noticed again today how I get depressed right away when people, for whatever reason, are not <u>very</u>, not <u>especially</u> friendly to me. I asked myself: why do I get so ill-humored about this? & answered myself: "Because I am quite unstable." Then the comparison oc-

---

237. The German word *"Himmel"* refers to both heaven and sky. One could also have translated "hover in heaven."

238. Wittgenstein first wrote "human love," struck "human," and continued with "love, human love." The German *"Liebe zum Vollkommenen"* is ambiguous: While it could be rendered "love of the perfect," the context suggests that Wittgenstein speaks of loving the perfect one (*den Vollkommenen*).

239. This sentence in quotation marks (*Alles andere findet sich*) may be a slightly misremembered or adapted quotation from Wilhelm Busch's *Eduards Traum* (p. 84): ". . . nur wer ein Herz hat, kann so recht fühlen und sagen, und zwar von Herzen, daß er nichts taugt. Das weitere findet sich [Things will sort themselves out]." Engelmann reports in his memoir that this latter line was one of Wittgenstein's favorites (*Letters from Ludwig Wittgenstein*, p. 116, note 1), so it makes sense that he might quote it (or a version of it) in his diary, without reference. [Gabriel Citron noted this allusion.]

Compare this passage to a remark from MS 120 (dated December 12, 1937) in *Culture and Value*, pp. 33/38f. Wittgenstein asks how the certainty is attainable that is requisite for salvation or redemption: "Only *love* can believe the resurrection. Or: what believes in resurrection is *love*. One might say: redeeming love believes even in the resurrection; holds fast even to the resurrection. [. . .] So this can only come about if you no longer support yourself on this earth but suspend yourself from heaven. Then *everything* is different and it is 'no wonder' if you can then do what now you cannot do. (Someone who is suspended is of course to be regarded like someone who is standing but the interplay of forces within him is quite different, after all & hence he is able to do quite different things than can one who stands.)" [I.S.]

curred to me that I feel just like a <u>bad</u> rider on a horse: if the horse is well disposed, then it goes well, but as soon as the horse gets restless, the rider becomes insecure, and <u>notices</u> his insecurity & that he depends entirely on the horse. I believe this is also how my sister Helene fares with people. Such a person is inclined to think well of people at one time, ill at another, depending on whether they are more or less friendly to her just then.[240]

9.4.[37]

"You must love the perfect one more than anything, then you are blessed."[241] This seems to me the sum of the Christian doctrine.

11.4.[37]

The ice is already bad now & I must take the boat across the river. This brings inconveniences & (small) dangers with it. I get faint-hearted & scared easily.

I plan to travel to Vienna in the first days of May. At the end of May to England.[242]

At around dawn I dreamt today that I had a long philosophical discussion with several others.

In it I arrived at a sentence which upon awakening I still vaguely knew.

"But let us talk in our mother tongue, & not believe that we must pull ourselves out of the swamp by our own hair;[243] that was—thank God—only a dream, after all. We are only supposed to remove misunderstandings, after all." I think, this is a <u>good</u> sentence.[244]

To God alone be praise!

---

240. Cf. Wittgenstein's account of his troubles with Anna Rebni, a neighbor in Skjolden (MS 119, 119r–121r; November 1937), where he finally asks after her coldness toward him only to find it was due to her (understandable) misunderstanding of his shaking his walking stick at her in a seemingly threatening way—apparently meant by him to be an expression of affection. (!!?)

241. See Matthew 22:37, Luke 10:27, and Mark 12:30. [I.S.]

242. Wittgenstein did indeed travel to Vienna in the first days of May, leaving from there to Cambridge on June 2. There he dictated a revised version of the *Philosophical Investigations* (TS 220). On August 10, he began his return to Skjolden, where he arrived on August 16 and stayed until the middle of December. [I.S.]

243. Wittgenstein is here referring to the fictional Baron Munchhausen's legendary feat of pulling himself (horse and rider) out of a swamp by pulling at his own hair.

244. Compare §91 of the *Philosophical Investigations*, also §§87, 90, 93, 109, 111, and 120; and the preface to the *Tractatus Logico-Philosophicus*.

The shortness of an expression: the shortness of an expression is not to be measured with a yard-stick. Some expressions are <u>shorter</u> that are <u>longer</u> on paper. Just as it is easier to write 'f' like <u>this</u>:

f rather than like <u>this</u>: f. One often feels that a sentence is too long & then wants to shorten it by striking out words; through that it assumes a forced & unsatisfying shortness. But perhaps it lacks words to have the right shortness.

16.4.[37]

Since yesterday the birches have had small green tips.—I have been feeling a bit unwell for a few days already, also <u>very</u> weary. I am working badly even though I make an effort. Am not clear how much sense it makes to stay here for another 14 days. A voice tells me: "why don't you travel earlier!" & another says: wait & stay!—If only I knew what is right!

In the last days I have often read in "Emperor & Galilean,"[245] & greatly impressed.—

Several things speak in favor of a departure; but also cowardice. And a few things also in favor of staying—but also pedantry, fear of the judgement of others, & the like.—It is not right to run away, to give in to impatience & cowardice, & on the other hand it seems unreasonable, & once again cowardly to stay here.

If I stay here, I am afraid of becoming sick & then not getting home & to England: as if I couldn't get sick or have an accident also in Vienna etc.!

It is <u>harder</u> to stay here than to leave.

17.4.[37]

Is being alone with oneself—or with God, not like being alone with a wild animal? It can attack you any moment.—But isn't that precisely why you shouldn't run away?! Isn't that, so to speak, what's glorious?! Doesn't it mean: grow fond of this wild animal!—And yet one must ask: Lead us not into temptation!

19.4.[37]

I believe: the word "believing" has wrought horrible havoc in religion. All the knotty thoughts about the "paradox" of the <u>eternal</u>

---

245. The Norwegian playwright Henrik Ibsen wrote *Emperor and Galilean* in 1873. The play examines the reign of Roman Emperor Julian the Apostate.

meaning of a <u>historical</u> fact and the like.[246] But if instead of "belief in Christ" you would say: "love of Christ," the paradox vanishes, that is, the irritation of the <u>intellect</u>. What does religion have to do with such a tickling of the intellect. (For someone or another this too may belong to their religion.)

It is not that now one could say: Yes, finally everything is simple—or intelligible. Nothing at all is <u>intelligible</u>, it is just not <u>unintelligible</u>.—

20.4.[37]

Last night & in the early morning almost all of the ice at the lake was driven down to the river so that the lake is almost entirely clear.

For a few months now I have been having blood in my stool again & also have some pain.—Think often that perhaps I will die of rectal cancer.[247] Be that as it may—would that I die <u>good</u>![248]

Feeling a bit sick & my thoughts aren't gaining momentum. In spite of warmth & good weather.

Today I am doing something wrong & bad: namely I vegetate. I can't seem to do anything sensible & am moreover in a sort of dull fear.—Under such circumstances I should perhaps fast & pray;—but I am inclined to eat & eat—for on a day like this I am afraid to look at myself.

Have directed myself to leave on May 1st—God willing.

23.4.[37]

Today the wind is howling around the house which always gets to me. It scares & disturbs me.

I am making an effort to fight my sad & mean feelings; but my strength wears out so quickly.

---

246. See diary remarks from late 1931, p. 64, *supra*, and a remark from MS 120 (dated December 8 and 9, 1937) in *Culture and Value*, p. 32/37: "Christianity is not based on a historical truth, but presents us with a (historical) report & says: now believe! But not believe this report with the belief that belongs to a historical report,—but rather: believe, through thick & thin & you can do this only as the outcome of a life. <u>Here you have a report!</u>—<u>don't relate to it as to another historical report!</u> Let it take a <u>quite different</u> place in your life.—There is nothing <u>paradoxical</u> in that! [. . .] Human beings seize this report (the gospels) believingly (that is, lovingly): <u>That</u> is the certainty of this taking-for-true; nothing <u>else</u>." [I.S.]

247. Wittgenstein had been repeatedly examined for a possibly serious intestinal disease when, in November 1949, he was diagnosed with cancer of the prostate. He died on April 29, 1951.

248. The German is ambiguous; while he may be wishing to die good (that is, as a good person), his expression can also be translated: "would that I die <u>well</u>."

26.4.[37]

Glorious weather. The birches are in leaf already. Last night I saw the first great Northern Lights. I looked at them for roughly 3 hours; an indescribable spectacle.

I <u>often</u> catch myself being shabby & miserly!!

27.4.[37]

You should love the truth: but you always love other things & the truth only on the side!

29.4.[37]

Somehow my thoughts are now <u>curdling</u> when I try to think about philosophy.[249]—Is that the end of my philosophical career?

30.4.[37]

I bear grudges to the highest degree. A <u>bad</u> sign.

> Wittgenstein left Norway in May, spending the summer in Vienna and then in Cambridge. Wittgenstein returned to Skjolden in August. Francis Skinner was staying with him for ten days while these last remarks were written. Compare Monk's biography, pp. 376f.; also *Wittgenstein and Norway*, p. 50.

24.9.37

Jews! for the longest time you haven't given the world anything for which it is grateful to you. And that, not because it is ungrateful. Since one doesn't feel gratitude for every contribution just because it is useful to us.

So give the world something for which you deserve not cold recognition but warm <u>gratitude</u>.

But the only thing it needs from you is your submission to fate.

You might give it roses that will blossom, never wilt.[250]

---

249. "Philosophy" replaces "logic."

250. Compare this remark by Wittgenstein's biographer Ray Monk (which was written before these diaries became known): "So long as he lived, Wittgenstein never ceased to struggle against his own pride, and to express doubts about his philosophical achievement and his own moral decency. After 1931, however, he dropped the language of anti-Semitism as a means of expressing those doubts" (p. 317). See also David Stern's "Was Wittgenstein a Jew?" (pp. 237–72).

One is right to fear the spirits[251] even of great men. And also those of <u>good</u> people. For what produced well-being in him[252] can effect ill-being in me. For the spirit without the <u>person</u> is not good—nor bad. But in me it can be a nasty spirit.

This last entry of the diary apparently filled its last remaining space. Wittgenstein left Norway in December 1937 and, in the course of 1938, returned once again to academic life in Cambridge. He returned to Norway only once more for a short visit in 1950.

---

251. "*Geister*" could be translated "minds," "spirits," or "ghosts."
252. The referent of "him" is unclear—someone or one of the great men or good people.

Appendix

Wittgenstein's Correspondence with Ludwig Hänsel

We have included several letters involving Ludwig Hänsel (1886–1959). Hänsel was a fellow prisoner of war with Wittgenstein after World War I, imprisoned in Cassino, Italy, from November 1918 through August 1919. During this time, they became friends, and then after the war, when Wittgenstein was an elementary school teacher, Hänsel was his supervisor. Their correspondence runs from 1919 until Wittgenstein's death in 1951.[1] In this brief appendix, we have included only a couple letters of general interest and then six letters that directly pertain to Wittgenstein's infamous confessions, as they throw particular light on Wittgenstein's comments in his diary from November 1936.

---

1. Their full correspondence has been published in the original German in *Ludwig Hänsel—Ludwig Wittgenstein: Eine Freundschaft*, and a selection of forty letters from 1929–1940 were republished with English translation in *Public and Private Occasions*, pp. 260–327. See also the preface to that selection (pp. 257–59) for a fuller account of Hänsel and Wittgenstein's friendship.

181   WITTGENSTEIN TO HÄNSEL

[Cambridge, after January 18, 1929]

L.H.!

You probably heard from my sister Gretl that I will be staying in Cambridge.[2] For the time being I am having a lot of trouble because I have not yet found a fitting & cheap apartment. The people are very nice to me & that does me good. My brain is rather dumb, hopefully that will improve soon. Write how all of you are doing! Please communicate also to Drobil[3] what is worth knowing about my worthy person & best regards to him. He is now rid of me until about March 20th. Then I'll come until around April 14th to Vienna.

For the time being my address is tentatively

L.W. c/o J.M. Keynes Esq.
King's College
Cambridge England

Once I know more, I will write more. Greetings to your children & your wife,

Yours
Wittgenstein

today I received a forwarded letter from Father Neururer.[4] He sends greetings.

---

2. Wittgenstein had planned to travel to Cambridge in the fall of 1928. Because of a cold, he postponed the trip until January 1929. He arrived on the 18th, intending to stay for only about fourteen days. This then became a permanent stay. During the first two weeks or so, he lived with Frank Plumpton and Lettice Ramsey at Mortimer Road 4, then with Mrs. Dobbs. [I.S.]

3. While prisoners of war, Wittgenstein and Hänsel formed a friendship with the Viennese sculptor Michael Drobil (1877–1958). Drobil made pencil sketches and a marble bust of Wittgenstein. Wittgenstein worked in Drobil's studio and, between 1926 and 1928, created the bust of a girl's head, which may have been modelled on Marguerite Respinger. See Wittgenstein's 1931 remark on this bust in *Culture and Value*, p. 19/16. [I.S.]

4. Alois Lucius Neururer (1878–1952) was ordained to the priesthood in 1904. He moved to Trattenbach as of December 12, 1917, and became the parish priest on May 1, 1918. Wittgenstein met Neururer while teaching at the Trattenbach elementary school from 1924 to 1926. Their friendship lasted to the end of their lives. The letters from Neururer are currently not accessible. Wittgenstein told Drury in a 1949 conversation (*Recollections of Wittgenstein*, p. 168): "I have had a letter from an old friend in Austria, a priest. In it he says he hopes my work will go well, if it should be God's will. Now that's all I want: if it should be God's will." [I.S.]

214 WITTGENSTEIN TO HÄNSEL

[Cambridge, after May 29, 1935]
Thursday

Dear Hänsel,

Many thanks for your letter. My plans for the summer and the future are still entirely unclear. I am still far from knowing whether they will even let me into Russia permanently.[5] I must still get advice from various sources, on the one hand about what to do in order to be let into Russia as a non-tourist, on the other hand about what sort of position or work I should try to get. I am also still unclear whether or not I should prepare myself here for this work through some sort of studies.[6] It is extraordinarily difficult to get intelligent & authoritative advice about this & just as difficult for me to arrive at a (in my sense) right decision. It is almost certain that I will not travel to Russia this summer but only in September.—But I see that it is quite impossible for me to explain to you—in a letter all the various possibilities & reasons & counter-arguments. Once I know more you'll hear it from me. I don't know yet and probably won't know for a month whether I will come to Austria in the summer.

Best regards, greetings to Drobil, your children & your dear wife. I am sure that all of you mourned for my aunt Clara.[7]

Yours
Ludwig Wittgenstein

---

5. Several times Wittgenstein contemplated traveling to Russia and settling down there (see, e.g., diary entry for April 4, 1937; p. 102, *supra*). He seriously pursued this option in 1935. After John Maynard Keynes had arranged an interview with the Russian ambassador, Wittgenstein left for Russia in September (see Wittgenstein's correspondence with Keynes in *Wittgenstein in Cambridge*, pp. 244–47). He stayed for only about two weeks, probably because he was offered a university position and not one as a worker on a collective farm (see Monk, pp. 350–52). [I.S.]

6. Wittgenstein had started to learn Russian from Fania Pascal in 1934 (see her memoir in *Recollections of Wittgenstein*). [I.S.]

7. Clara Wittgenstein had died on May 29, 1935, in Laxenburg (and see diary entry for October 2, 1930; p. 28, *supra*). [I.S.]

220 WITTGENSTEIN TO HÄNSEL

[Cambridge, after June 22, 1936
Thursday at present]

Dear Hänsel!

Many thanks for your dear letter. I am very glad that Drobil is taking on Mareile. It will do her (and him) good. I will stay here for another month & then go to Norway (or perhaps Iceland) in order to work there.[8] I would like to spend about a year there in peace, but, if possible, want to come to Vienna for Christmas. How it will go there (in Norway) with my work, God knows.—You will have heard of Schlick getting shot at the University.[9] How terrible!

My address for the time being is "Trinity College." Let me hear from you not too long from now. Best regards from me to your children & your wife & also to Drobil, the old D.-S.[10]

Your old friend

Ludwig Wittgenstein

---

8. On August 8, 1936, Wittgenstein left for Norway and as of August 27 settled in his cabin there (see the entries in his diary, beginning November 19, 1936; p. 68, *supra*). He worked on a German version of the so-called *Brown Book*. After abandoning it, he started with the first draft of the *Philosophical Investigations*. He left for Vienna on December 8, went to Cambridge in January, and returned to Norway at the end of that month. Excepting one other interruption (from May to August in Vienna and Cambridge), he stayed there until the middle of December 1937. [I.S.]

9. Moritz Schlick was killed on June 22, 1936, by his former doctoral student, thirty-three-year-old Hans Nelbök. His stated reasons concerned Schlick's hedonism and his empiricist critique of all transcendental or metaphysical knowledge. Nelbök was sentenced to ten years in prison but after two years of imprisonment was released immediately after the National Socialists seized power in Austria. [I.S.] In a letter to Wittgenstein dated July 11, 1936, his sister Margarete writes (*Wittgenstein's Family Letters*, pp. 208–9): "Waismann . . . called me (although I didn't know who he was) & said he wanted to speak to me about something concerning Schlick. . . . He wanted to ask me whether you might be willing to accept a teaching position in Vienna . . ."

10. "D.-S." stands for "*Drecksau* [filthy swine]" in German but also suggests the corresponding term of endearment "dumb shit." Compare Wittgenstein's April/May 1936 letter to his sister Helene in *Wittgenstein's Family Letters*, p. 205. There he sends regards to her husband Max—"the old D.S." [I.S.]

225 WITTGENSTEIN TO HÄNSEL

[Skjolden] 7.11.36.

Dear Hänsel!

I lied to you & several others back then during the Italian intern-ment when I said that I was descended one quarter from Jews and three quarters from Arians, even though it is just the other way round.[11] This cowardly lie has burdened me for a long time & like <u>many</u> other lies I also told this one to others. Until today I did not find the strength to confess it.[12]—I hope you will forgive me; yes I even hope that you will continue to deal with me & as before & won't like me the less. I know that is expecting <u>much</u>, but I hope for it nevertheless. I have to apologize to you also for several other lies.—I wish that you will make this letter known to your dear wife & the children, to my siblings & their children, to Drobil & my other friends & Mrs. Sjögren; that is, that you let them read it. <u>May all of them forgive me, too</u>; I know that I am causing you & everyone <u>great pain</u> & yet I must do it. I am afraid that perhaps some will not be <u>able</u> to forgive me entirely. I don't want to write anymore today. Fare well!

Yours
Ludwig Wittgenstein

I am doing well.

226 HÄNSEL TO WITTGENSTEIN

Vienna, 15. Nov. 36.

Dear Wittgenstein!

You are (again and again) a marvelous human being![13] Your let-ter moved me very much and gladdened me greatly, for you and for me. (<u>I</u> thank you for your confidence.) As far as the one quarter of Jewish blood is concerned, while I hadn't doubted your words, I

---

11. This is the confession Wittgenstein mentions in his diary entry for November 19, 1936; p. 68, *supra*. It is the only known written record of the series of confessions Wittgenstein made in 1936 and 1937 (recipients included G. E. Moore, Francis Skin-ner, Rowland Hutt, Maurice O'C. Drury, Paul Engelmann, and Fania Pascal). [I.S.]

12. Wittgenstein uses "*gestehen*," that is, a word without religious connotation that refers to the admission of a crime or deed.

13. On November 21, 1936, Wittgenstein records his reaction to this letter in his diary; p. 70, *supra*.

have known at least—forgive me!—that it is harder for you than for other people to acknowledge your own defects. And I, by the way, can't do it either. You have often spoken of it yourself and—during the internment—added rightly: that others with their forthrightness in small matters are less forthright than you with your great lies, or something like that. (I counted myself among those others and have reason enough to do it all the more so now.) But you make all well again in such a grand manner. (If only I could help bring about <u>that you would really go to confession.</u>[14] Could you acquaint yourself with Sigrid Undset, in Norway? With her personally. You too would get something out of her novel The Master of Hestviken, I believe.)[15]

Initially I meant to follow your instructions to make the letter known to my family, your siblings and the others mentioned by you. Under the impression of your letter. And with the conviction, which I still hold, that they would be just as happy about it as I. I would have gladly shared their joy with mine and (for example) liked to have seen my children moved by it. But I am not doing it after all. I don't have the strength for it. Not even if you asked me to do it. I could speak about it some time later in the future, in your honor. But to make the content of the letter known now, to read it to others, to send it around, this you must not demand from me. Don't be angry at my refusal! (Also don't be angry that I referred to religious confession or, for that matter, to Sigrid Undset!) It happens (both of it) out of friendship. I admire you. But I like you, too, simply as another human being and from my heart. It goes without saying that you have faults, and I haven't talked myself out of those. I am too soberly inclined for that. I have mine, too (and far more miserable ones than you). That you like me anyhow and trust me, is part of my good luck. That you don't accept this and that in me, pains me. But that pain is healthy. It protects me (as Karl Kraus has protected me here and there) against conceit. It brought about that again and again I have remained fairly sober also toward myself.

But since I have already begun talking about myself: we have moved into the five echoing halls, furnishing them slowly, but have

---

14. Hänsel speaks of *"beichten"* here, that is, of confession in the religious, especially Catholic sense.

15. The Norwegian writer Sigrid Undset (1882–1949) received the Nobel prize for literature in 1928, especially for her novel *Kristin Lavransdatter* (1920–1922). In 1924, she converted to Catholicism, and from 1925 to 1927, she wrote *Olav Andunssøn* (translated as *The Master of Hestviken*), a stark and violent tale of love and guilt, selflessness and pride. [I.S.]

remained to this day (my wife even now doesn't really want to leave it) in the small room in which we made our nest at the very beginning. I am including a card for you.

All the best for your work and for your heart! for your soul.

Yours
Ludwig Hänsel

227   WITTGENSTEIN TO HÄNSEL

[Skjolden] 22. Nov. [1936 Saturday]

Dear Hänsel,

Just a few words in a hurry. Heartfelt thanks for your dear & good letter which I haven't deserved by any means. But that you don't want to forward my letter is a heavy blow. For now I must write to the others, for know it they <u>must</u>! Yes this is all the harder since in about 3 weeks, when I come to Austria I must make a more comprehensive confession[16] & I hoped that my letter would prepare the ground for this; to make it easier that way <u>for the others</u> & also for me. After all, I didn't want that you read them the letter, just that you pass it on; first for example to my sister Mining[17] so that <u>she</u> can then do the rest.

I want to close now.

I am as always

Yours
Ludwig Wittgenstein

---

16. Wittgenstein again speaks of "*Geständnis*," that is, of a secular confession of guilt.
17. "Mining" is Hermine Wittgenstein. [I.S.]

228   HÄNSEL TO WITTGENSTEIN

Vienna, 26.11.36

Dear Wittgenstein!

You are right. I am passing your letter on to your sister. Suddenly I see that I am allowed to do this and that I can help you through this. You must forgive my uncertainty.

All the best!

Yours
Hänsel

I will also read the letter to my children and my wife.

229   WITTGENSTEIN TO HÄNSEL

[Skjolden, 30.11.1936] Monday

Dear Hänsel

Thank you for your letter. But you rendered me a <u>great</u> service through your refusal to pass on my letter. For I saw that I would now <u>have to</u> write down my <u>whole</u> confession.[18] For initially I had believed that I couldn't do this.—I sent it about 6 days ago to my sister Mining. It is meant for all my relatives & friends & you will therefore receive it, too.[19]

May you forgive me also what you will be reading there!

About religious confession[20] & the Norwegian author I want to talk to you when I come to Vienna. I want to arrive between the 12th & the 15th & <u>joyfully</u> anticipate seeing everyone again, even if fear is mixed in with my joy.

In Vienna I will be very much in need of your help.

I am doing very well.

Yours
Ludwig Wittgenstein

---

18. Wittgenstein uses the secular *"Geständnis"* again.
19. According to Arvid Sjögren, this version of Wittgenstein's confession was placed in the reading room of the Wittgenstein family. Not everyone chose to read it, see the following letter from Hermine to Hänsel, p. 119, *infra*. [I.S.]
20. "Religious confession" is a translation of *"Beichte."*

231 HERMINE WITTGENSTEIN TO HÄNSEL

[Vienna, before December 11, 1936[21]]

Dear Headmaster

Enclosed is the Christmas present for the "children," they must then, as always, present the results on the first holiday.[22]

Just now I received a cable from Ludwig, saying that he is coming Friday evening. I am so glad that I pursued the matter like this, only Engelmann is missing now, whose address I don't have yet, and those mentioned who live in America about whom my sister Stonborough still wants to talk to Ludwig. I am very curious about his mood; I believe the affection will have increased of all those who have read the confession, or refused it or requested it for later;[23] but it takes <u>two</u> persons for a contact, it depends on how Ludwig reacts. With best regards, dear headmaster,

H. Wittgenstein

---

21. Wittgenstein left Skjolden for Vienna on December 8, 1936. The dating of this letter is based on the assumption that his cable is announcing his arrival from Norway on Friday evening, December 11. (It is also possible, however, that Wittgenstein cabled Hermine that he is accepting her invitation to an event that she has organized for a Friday evening after his arrival.)

22. Much of Hermine and Gretl's correspondence with Hänsel concerns monetary and other gifts and stipends to him and his three children, at this point between eighteen and twenty-two years of age. The annual Christmas visit probably included a musical recital or the like.

23. On December 3, 1936, Wittgenstein's sister Margarete Stonborough wrote to him: "My dear, my good Luki, I am grateful that I can for once say: I think of you with tender love. I do it often, but I haven't ever dared say it. If your confession has brought you some relief, then I am grateful to God that he has made it possible for you to make it. . . . Surely you know that I could counter every one of your confessed sins with the same or ones far worse in kind" (*Wittgenstein's Family Letters*, p. 211).

Works Cited

Alice Ambrose, ed., *Wittgenstein's Lectures: Cambridge, 1932–1935* (Totowa, NJ: Rowman & Littlefield, 1979).

Ludwig Boltzmann, "On a Thesis of Schopenhauer," in *Theoretical Physics and Philosophical Problems*, ed., B. McGuinness (Dordrecht, Netherlands: D. Reidel, 1974).

O. K. Bouwsma, *Wittgenstein: Conversations 1949–1951* (Indianapolis, IN: Hackett, 1986).

Karl Britton, "Recollections of Ludwig Wittgenstein," *Cambridge Journal*, vol. 7, 1954, pp. 709–15.

Wilhelm Busch, *Eduards Traum* (Munich: F. Bassermann, 1891).

M. Drury, "Conversations with Wittgenstein," in *Recollections of Wittgenstein*, ed., R. Rhees (Oxford: Oxford University Press, Revised edition 1984).

Sigmund Freud, *General Introduction to Psychoanalysis* (New York: Pocket Book, 1953).

Ludwig Hänsel and Ludwig Wittgenstein, *Ludwig Hänsel—Ludwig Wittgenstein: Eine Freundschaft, Briefe Aufsätze Kommentare*, eds., I. Somavilla, et al. (Innsbruck, Austria: Haymon Verlag, 1994).

William James, *The Varieties of Religious Experience* (New York: Penguin, 1982).

K. Johannessen, et al., eds., *Wittgenstein and Norway* (Oslo: Folum, 1994).

Søren Kierkegaard, "The Jewel on Thin Ice," in *The Parables of Kierkegaard*, ed., T. Oden (Princeton, NJ: Princeton University Press, 1978).

Søren Kierkegaard, *Repetition: An Essay in Experimental Psychology* (New York: Harper and Row, 1964).

John King, "Recollections of Wittgenstein," in *Recollections of Wittgenstein*, ed., R. Rhees (Oxford: Oxford University Press, Revised edition 1984).

Karl Kraus, *The Last Days of Mankind*, trs., F. Bridgham and E. Timms (New Haven, CT: Yale University Press, 2015).

Desmond Lee, ed., *Wittgenstein's Lectures: Cambridge, 1930–1932* (Totowa, NJ: Rowman & Littlefield, 1980).

Norman Malcolm, *Ludwig Wittgenstein: A Memoir* (Oxford: Oxford University Press, New edition 1984).

Brian McGuinness, *Wittgenstein: A Life, The Young Ludwig* (Berkeley, CA: University of California Press, 1988).

Moses Mendelssohn, *Gesammelte Schriften* (Leipzig: Brockhaus, 1844).

Karl Menger, *Reminiscences of the Vienna Circle and the Mathematical Colloquium*, eds., L. Golland, et al. (Dordrecht, Netherlands: Kluwer, 1994).

Cheryl Misak, *Frank Ramsey: A Sheer Excess of Powers* (Oxford: Oxford University Press, 2020).

Ray Monk, *Ludwig Wittgenstein: The Duty of Genius* (New York: Free Press, 1990).

G. E. Moore, *Wittgenstein: Lectures, Cambridge 1930–1933*, eds., D. Stern, et al. (Cambridge: Cambridge University Press, 2016).

Friedrich Nietzsche, "The Antichrist," in *The Portable Nietzsche*, ed., W. Kaufmann (New York: Penguin, 1976).

———, *Philosophy in the Tragic Age of the Greeks*, tr., M. Cowan (Washington, DC: Gateway, 1996).

Alfred Nordmann, "The Sleepy Philosopher: How to Read Wittgenstein's Diaries," in *Wittgenstein: Biography and Philosophy*, ed., J. Klagge (Cambridge: Cambridge University Press, 2001).

Fania Pascal, "A Personal Memoir," in *Recollections of Wittgenstein*, ed., R. Rhees (Oxford: Oxford University Press, Revised edition 1984).

Richard Raatzsch, ed., *Goethe and Wittgenstein—Seeing the World's Unity in Its Variety*, in *Wittgenstein-Studien* (Bern: Peter Lang, 2003).

Frank Ramsey, "Critical Notice: Review of the *Tractatus*," *Mind*, vol. 32. no. 128, October 1923, pp. 465–78.

Theodore Redpath, *Ludwig Wittgenstein: A Student's Memoir* (London: Duckworth, 1990).

Rush Rhees, "Preface," in *Recollections of Wittgenstein*, ed., R. Rhees (Oxford: Oxford University Press, Revised edition 1984).

Hans Rochelt, "*Das Creditiv der Sprache*," *Literatur und Kritik*, vol. 33, April 1969, pp. 169–76.

Josef G. F. Rothhaupt and Aidan Seery, "*Ludwig Wittgenstein war ein 'Stern' in meinem Leben*"—Interview mit Marguerite de Chambrier," *Wittgenstein-Jahrbuch 2000* (Book 1), eds. W. Lütterfelds, et al. (Bern: Peter Lang, 2001).

Bertrand Russell, *Autobiography of Bertrand Russell, vol. 2: 1914–1944* (Boston: Little, Brown, 1968).

Oliver Sacks, *The Man Who Mistook His Wife for a Hat* (New York: Summit Books, 1985).

Arthur Schopenhauer, *Parerga and Paralipomena* (Oxford: Clarendon, 1974).

———, *The World as Will and Representation*, tr., E. Payne (New York: Dover, 1966).

Ilse Somavilla and B. Sieradzka-Baziur, eds., *Wittgenstein's* Denkbewegungen *(Diaries 1930–1932/1936–1937): Interdisciplinary Perspectives* (Innsbruck, Austria: Studien Verlag, 2019).

Oswald Spengler, *The Decline of the West*, vols. 1 and 2 (New York: Knopf, 1957).

Benedict Spinoza, *Collected Works*, ed., E. Curley (Princeton, NJ: Princeton University Press, 1985).

David Stern, "Was Wittgenstein a Jew?" in *Wittgenstein: Biography and Philosophy*, ed., J. Klagge (Cambridge: Cambridge University Press, 2001).

J. P. Stern, *Lichtenberg: A Doctrine of Scattered Occasions* (Bloomington, IN: Indiana University Press, 1959).

Bela Szabados, *Wittgenstein as Philosophical Tone-Poet: Philosophy and Music in Dialogue* (New York: Rodopi, 2014).

Leo Tolstoy, *The Gospel in Brief: The Life of Jesus*, tr., Dustin Condren (New York: Harper Perennial, 2011).

Heinrich von Kleist, *Hermannsschlacht* (Berlin: Holzinger, 2016).

G. H. von Wright, "Georg Christoph Lichtenberg als Philosoph," *Theoria*, vol. 8, no. 3, 1942, pp. 201–17.

Friedrich Waismann, *Wittgenstein and the Vienna Circle*, ed., B. McGuinness (Oxford: Blackwell, 1979).

W. H. Watson, *On Understanding Physics* (Cambridge: Cambridge University Press, 1938).

Otto Weininger, *Sex and Character: An Investigation of Fundamental Principles*, ed., D. Steuer, tr., L. Löb (Indianapolis, IN: Indiana University Press, 2005).

Hermine Wittgenstein, "My Brother Ludwig," in *Recollections of Wittgenstein*, ed., R. Rhees (New York: Oxford University Press, Revised edition 1984).

———, *Familienerinnerungen*, ed., I. Somavilla (Innsbruck: Haymon, 2015).

Ludwig Wittgenstein, *Culture and Value*, ed., G. H. von Wright, tr., P. Winch (Chicago: University of Chicago Press, 1980 / Oxford: Blackwell, Revised Second edition 1998).

———, *Denkbewegungen: Tagebücher, 1930–1932/1936–1937*, ed., Ilse Somavilla (Innsbruck, Austria: Haymon Verlag, 1997).

———, *Lectures and Conversations on Aesthetics, Psychology and Religious Belief*, ed., C. Barrett (Berkeley, CA: University of California Press, 1967).

———, *Letters from Ludwig Wittgenstein: With a Memoir*, ed., P. Engelmann (Oxford: Blackwell, 1967).

———, *Notebooks 1914–1916* (Oxford: Blackwell, Second edition 1979).

———, *Philosophical Investigations* (New York: Wiley Blackwell, Fourth edition 2009).

———, *Philosophical Occasions: 1912–1951*, eds., J. Klagge and A. Nordmann (Indianapolis, IN: Hackett, 1993).

———, *Philosophical Remarks*, ed., R. Rhees (Oxford: Basil Blackwell, 1975).

———, *Public and Private Occasions*, eds., J. Klagge and A. Nordmann (Lanham, MD: Rowman & Littlefield, 2003).

———, *Private Notebooks: 1914–1916*, tr., M. Perloff (New York: Liveright, 2022).

———, *Remarks of the Foundations of Mathematics* (Cambridge, MA: MIT Press, Revised edition 1978).

———, *Tractatus Logico-Philosophicus* (New York: Routledge, 1961).

———, *Wiener Ausgabe*, vols. 2–4, ed. M. Nedo (Vienna: Springer, 1994–1995).

———, *Wittgenstein in Cambridge: Letters and Documents, 1911–1951*, ed., B. McGuinness (Oxford: Blackwell, 2008).

———, *Wittgenstein's Family Letters*, ed., B. McGuinness, tr. P. Winslow (London: Bloomsbury, 2019).

Ludwig Wittgenstein and Rudolf Koder, *Wittgenstein und die Musik: Ludwig Wittgenstein—Rudolf Koder Briefwechsel*, ed., M. Alber (Innsbruck: Haymon, 2000).

Index